What Others Are Saying about This Book...

"Since I often find myself in a state of overwhelm while juggling family and business, I was thrilled when I heard that Debra was putting her secrets into book form. Who better to learn from than a woman who runs triathlons, invests in real estate, writes books, does non-profit work, creates millionaire mindsets, is 100% present for her family and always seems to have a smile on her face?" —**Debra Halperin, Yes to Success, Inc.**

"At a time when today's culture holds up contradictory—and humanly impossible—ideals for working mothers, this book is a much-needed return to sanity. The positive, inspiring and realistic message is exactly what working moms need to create financial—and personal—success." —**Gail Z. Martin, DreamSpinner Communications**

"Ambitious mothers can run a business and raise a family and be more relaxed, have more energy, and be more fulfilled by reading this ground-breaking book." —**Peggy McColl, New York Times Best-Selling Author of** *Your Destiny Switch*

"The demands of motherhood, coupled with extraordinary success as an entrepreneur - takes courage, stamina and a deep passion for your business mission. Debra Kasowski guides you intuitively to integrate home and business. This book takes you deep. I highly recommend." —**Shawne Duperon, 6-Time EMMY® winning media coach, ShawneTV**

"Reading this book is like getting a sneak peek inside the hearts and minds of many women today, women who are seeking something meaningful for their lives while raising their families. If you are ready to learn how to follow your dream and still be a good mom, this book is a must read." —**April Morris (Seen on Season 2 of ABC's Hit TV show Shark Tank, FOX News & LA Times)**

"Wow! A must read for every entrepreneurial woman who truly wants more. Both inspirational and strategy filled, this book will show you how to build the business of your dreams while keeping the family you so love." —**Michele Scism, Decisive Minds, LLC**

"Debra has captured the essence that every entrepreneurial mom can build a business and still serve the family she loves. You must not only be passionate about what you want in life but you also need to take action to turn it into reality, make more money, serve others and truly love what you do." —**Lori Raudnask, Author of *Persistence Pays: How Getting What You Want Is Easier Than You Think***

"Enjoying success at home as well as in business can be tough double act to achieve. This easy-to-follow guide shows you HOW, but even more importantly, helps you figure out your WHY. This is a great resource for our greatest natural resource—the Entrepreneurial Mom!" —**Dr. Ganz Ferrance, Registered Psychologist, President –The Ferrance Group**

"This book will be your number one resource if you are currently juggling entrepreneurship and raising a family. Debra shares savvy tips, smart advice and easy-to-follow advice that will help you create a life that you truly love!" —**Jessica Swanson, Shoestring Marketing**

DEDICATION

For all of the courageous moms who want to make a difference in
the world with their God-given talents. The world is waiting for you
to step out of your comfort zone and into your greatness!
And, to my children Krista, Nathan, and Jordan:
You inspire me each day to give my best.
You are my "why" for doing what I do.
I love you more every day!

TABLE OF CONTENTS

FOREWORD

Every woman who has made the decision to own a business needs to read this book, plain and simple.

The past 30 years have been an incredible journey for me. It started when I married and became an instant step-mother to two fabulous young people. Instant motherhood!

I am no longer married to their father but having helped raised 2 stepchildren has been one of the greatest blessings of my life. They are amazing young adults now, parents to their own children—and my stepdaughter is now an entrepreneur.

The point of this introduction? Well, I, too, am an entrepreneurial Mom. Only for me, back then, there were no books no guides—no Dr. Phil, no Debra Kasowski, no help on the journey. And it was hard. Really hard.

My work included long business trips away from home. It included road trips up and down the Province. There were times when my husband and I crossed paths along the highway, handed over the dog, and then coordinated our schedules as to what hotel we would meet in later that night as, at the time, we were both on the road for our work. Then, when I arrived home, it was time to coordinate more schedules: child pick-up, activities, shopping, cooking, and so much more.

Yes, the life of an Entrepreneurial Mom!

I believe that, more than any other time in our history, this is THE time for women to succeed. This is the time for women to excel and to live their dreams. I am proof of that.

As a business coach, my work with women entrepreneurs led me to the amazing Debra Kasowski just over a year ago. I recognized the incredible talent she had and the God-given gifts she needed to share with the world. I also recognized that she needed help in doing that.

Debra is a true professional—she is the epitome of the working Mom—and she has a dream. What I love most about her is the undying devotion to her family and to her business. "The Entrepreneurial Mom's Guide to Growing a Business, Raising a Family, and Creating a Life You Love" is her brain child—and it is time to release it to the world. Women so desperately need the information that Debra has compiled in this book.

From personal examples of handling a certain Valentine's Day party to the generous sharing of resources, through to the powerful examples of what can happen when you actually apply what you learn in this book—it is a gold mine of information!

Debra has written this book as her contribution to the women's movement—a true labor of love, so that you do not have to go through the many challenges that I experienced all those years earlier.

This book is for you, the modern woman who is following her dream—who is running a business—who is raising a family—or wants to do all those things. This Guide gives you everything you need to know to get past the hurdles, to get organized, to stay on top of things, to find the right resources and to take care of YOU along the way.

I know it will stimulate thought, understanding and creative ideas about how you can take advantage of all that's sure to be happening in your life and in your business for years to come.

We can learn many things simply by reading and applying what you are doing in your business. It's all in here for the taking. If you're like most women, you're looking for the shortest, fastest way to get to the end result—without compromising on quality. That's the benefit of this book! Read it. You'll be glad you did.

I read the book and I learned a lot. Debra, on behalf of my entre-preneurial step-daughter, and for all the women out there, thank you for this great Guide.

Pat Mussieux
Founder, Wealthy Women Leaders
http://www.wealthywomenleaders.com
GOLD Stevie Award Winner - 2012 Female Entrepreneur of the Year in Canada

ACKNOWLEDGEMENTS

As I reflect on how the spark of an idea for this project came to be, I think of all the teachers and messengers that have entered into my life. People say that when the student is ready the teacher will appear. I am grateful for each one of those people for sharing their message at the right time so individuals like me can serve others in a bigger way.

I have been very blessed by God with incredible children (Krista, Nathan, and Jordan) and a supportive spouse, Stephen. I know there may have been times when you wondered where my brainstormed ideas would take me, and I thank you for keeping me grounded and for your patience as I focused on many hours of writing. Of course thanks go to my parents, John and Elizabeth, who have always reminded me that no matter what I set my mind to I can accomplish. Thank you for your unconditional love and for reminding me that people are waiting to hear my message. And thank you for encouraging me to always remain true to myself.

To my publisher, Bettie Youngs, thank you for believing in me and in an idea that sparked out of a late night brainstorming session and a leap of faith. Your enthusiasm and knowledge have made me see that there are stories everywhere. You are amazing!

To my editor, Elisabeth Rinaldi, working with you gets better every time. Words cannot convey how grateful I am for the magic that you create when editing a book. I have learned so much from you—you are a gift.

To my business coach, Pat Mussieux, thank you for seeing in me what I only dreamed for myself. You believed in me and my message from the get-go and encouraged me to stay on track and step up my game. You are a treasure.

To my co-author of *GPS Your Best Life*, Charmaine Hammond, writing my first book with you challenged me to dig deeper and give more. Thank you.

To my dear friends, Wendy Mandiuk, thank you for your loving lectures during our car travels. You knew that there was no way I could escape. Mariana Konsolos, thank you for late night talks in the driveway. At least I was the driver and could get away if I needed. Your words have ignited my flame even brighter. My dear friend Dianna Bowes thank you for the brainstorming sessions. You are shining stars!

To my Facebook friend to real-life friend, Stephen Welton, the Card Sending Cop with SendOutCards, you have demonstrated what gratitude and appreciation are really about. You, my friend, do not realize that greatness you possess.

Special thanks to my mentors that I met and those I have yet to meet. You have influenced and guided me during this entrepreneurial journey. I am forever grateful for the teachings of Jack Canfield in *The Success Principles* for his kind words of support and encouragement. Dan Lok and Darren Weeks for challenging me to step out of my comfort zone and to just do it—because I *will* figure it out. Brendon Burchard, Marcia Wieder, Darren Hardy, Debbie Mrazek, Kim Duke, Marie Forleo, Michele Scism, Lethia Owens, Sandra Yancey, Bob Burg, Suzanne Evans, and Larry Winget, your words of wisdom have inspired me.

Of course, I cannot forget about the Health Link Alberta staff who were my cheerleaders and supportive crew who silently and not so silently reminded me to live my purpose. You know who you are!

My coaching clients and *The Millionaire Woman* ladies who I serve: I love helping you realize your potential and get excited by all your wins! You deserve the best life has to offer!

This book would not have been written if it was not for all the moms in business who wanted the best for their families, business, and lives. I salute you for staking your claim in the marketplace.

Let's create the life *you* absolutely *love*!

INTRODUCTION

MY STORY

In October of 2007, I was sitting in the front row of a real estate presentation observing how the audience appeared mesmerized by the speaker. He was charismatic and knew his subject matter. During the break, I asked him if I could "pick his brain about becoming a speaker." That was mistake number one! He told me to hold my thought, and we would address it right after the break. He then brought me in front of 200 people and asked me what I had done wrong. I felt my face turning red. I told the audience what I had asked, and then it hit me…as I had just finished reading Robert Kiyosaki's book *Rich Dad, Poor Dad*. The book talked about "not picking the brain" but learning from a mentor and working for free or volunteering to learn what you need to learn. I realized I had been asking for the speaker's knowledge. Some people may think his approach was harsh. However, I took that moment as one of my greatest lessons. No sooner than I shared my question did people from the audience come to me and share how I could start reaching my dream.

I did not realize it that evening, but as I began to reflect a bit more, I remembered people in my life telling me that I was good at public speaking, I cared about people, and that my smile was contagious as I exuded happiness.

I once saw Oprah Winfrey live, and she talked about the common thread or "golden thread" that runs through our lives. The one you will discover as you reflect on all the key events that have brought you to where you are today. My reflection started to surface more and more virtues and strengths that I knew I could utilize. In school, I was president of junior and senior high student council and loved leadership. When I was eighteen, I was in a beauty pageant and my talent was public speaking. While at university, I facilitated workshops on interview skills and resume writing. In my management position, I coached nurses on their performance and helped them become more aware of their performance and practice.

In my speaking and coaching business, I continue to support women through facilitating networking nights, presenting workshops, coaching, and interviewing the experts. Because of all of my questioning, I have become known as the "facilitator of thought." Little did I know then, all of these events contributed to the person I am today. By doing this exercise, I know greater things are yet to come.

Now let's bring the kids into the picture. I am the type of mom who would pack them up and take all three kids under the age five to the swimming pool by herself. I would have two within arm's reach and the other in front of me on a float in the shallow lagoon. I do not see children as a hindrance as a lot of my social activity came from being around other moms. I would plan picnic lunches and go to the nearby playground so we could have some hands on time. When they entered school, I started keeping a color-coded calendar of activities for each family member and a binder with information for their respective activities.

If you want something to work and you plan for it, you can make it happen. It is truly a matter of perspective. Through the years I have had dozens of people ask me how I get so much done or tell me "I just do not know how you do it." I have read tons of books on motivation, business, and personal development. I have practically eliminated television from my life, unless I am ironing or having a family movie night. I've learned to recognize my priorities and where my time needs to go. I work from lists so I can stay focused on my goals and what I need to do to get them done.

When you become more aware of where you spend your time and are clear on what it is you wish to achieve, transformation can occur because your motivation and efforts are intrinsic. You do things for *you*! You become unstoppable.

Many of my friends and colleagues would ask me advice about their businesses, raising their families, and sometimes even about their relationships. I enjoy working with women because they are the influencers of tomorrow and they are the heart of the family. I know from experience the impact we can have when we chase after our dreams.

My *Millionaire Woman* concept was born of the saying "feeling like a million bucks"—when life has its moments of utopia. The tagline "rich from the inside out" followed. It all starts with *you*. Each woman can be a "millionaire woman." In my business, I aim to inspire and empower women to be rich in all areas of their lives so that they can then attract more business, ideal clients, and make more money while creating a life they love. I help them become more aware of the potential they have inside by helping them gain clarity on what they want, why they want it, and challenge them to get over the self-limiting beliefs that hold them back—the false concepts that keep replaying in their heads. I help them discover their purpose and mission so they can lead their lives from the heart and serve others in a bigger way. I believe that successful business women nurture relationships and collaborate with others to leverage their time, money, and resources so they can get the riches they deserve. The confidence these women exude is contagious and I love watching them flourish and share their love of life and riches with their families. When you feel like you are fulfilling your mission or purpose of why you were put on this earth, you feel like your feet have not touched the ground.

Since that ah-ha moment, mentors entered my life. I joined Toast-masters, and created products and wrote a book. At Toastmasters, I was told that they would evaluate me a little tougher than others (because I asked for it and they felt I was at a much higher level but needed to go through the competency levels.) I also joined the Canadian Speakers Association so I could learn more about the business of speaking. I learned many tips and techniques here and there. I also learned that I was a lot further ahead that I had thought. I kept telling myself I needed to do and learn more before taking action.

We can be a bit too critical on ourselves, don't you think? I am a person who pays attention to details and have tendencies of perfection. But I have learned very quickly that success comes from taking imperfect action and adjusting your path along the way. That is why it is so important to acknowledge our accomplishments and not just the tasks we cross off our to-do lists. You need to keep momentum by taking action steps.

I have been very fortunate to have a great support system and people around me who understand my goal and dream and want to support me. My husband will often say, "Don't you need to work on some of your business items. You go work on them and I will look after the kids." I have become more cognizant of where and how I spend my time. I have become an amazing time manager as I need to focus on my agenda to accomplish what I need to get done in the time that I have. There is definitely truth to Tim Ferris's book, *The Four Hour Work Week*, where he explains how you can get things done in a short period of time. You may have even heard the saying, "Do it, delegate it, or dump it." You can do it yourself, delegate it to someone else, or take it off your list all together as it may not be serving you. When I work from my list and see what needs to get done, I get laser focused in the amount of time that I have. You can get a lot done when you hold yourself accountable and to the standards you wish to abide by.

Now I want to take what I have learned through my reading, attending conferences, and through my business to help you to achieve the success you desire. You do not have to "pick my brain." I am here to lift you higher, share what I know has worked for me, and encourage you to take the tips and techniques that resonate with you and implement them so you can grow your business, raise your family your way, and create a life you absolutely love waking up to each day.

There comes a time in a woman's life where she asks herself "Who am I?" Often, this questioning crossroad is reached after she's married and has kids, when the outside world has started to define her identity as "someone's wife" or "someone's mom." This is not a place of crisis, but a place of transition, and after reflection we come to a realization that we have so much more to offer the world than perhaps we had initially thought and we can rediscover our authentic selves and what we truly want.

As a mother, you can become engrossed in your current role of juggling family duties while you work—or contemplate going back to work or starting your own business. This does not mean that you question motherhood, as it is such a joy to bring children into this world and watch them gain their independence. Mothers often suffer from "mommy guilt" where we feel guilty for wanting something for ourselves above and beyond our maternal obligations. Or maybe, you suffer in silence trying to be the devoted wife and mother and dedicated employee. You may have family and friends questioning you saying, "What is wrong with what you currently have? Why aren't you happy?" You may secretly wish you could have your own temper tantrum when you feel overwhelmed with your current state of affair. If the kids can have a temper tantrum, why can't you? Your passions may have changed, but you must not lose sight of what your purpose and dreams once were. It becomes increasingly important to regain your identity. What do you want for you?

A NEW BIRTH, A NEW BEGINNING

As if your life is not busy enough with sleepless nights, spilled milk, or shuttling your kids to and from activities, you've decided you want more. This *more* is not something you randomly picked out of the sky. It is a burning desire to create something for you, a burning desire that you have so much more to give to others around you. The voice inside you grew louder and louder finally decided to take action. You may be deciding to go into business or have already gotten one off the ground but feel like you are struggling to make things happen. Don't give up yet. Great things are coming your way!

To grow a business, raise a family, and create a life you love, you must remember what your dreams are and what you want for yourself and the next chapter of your life—the chapter that includes a business *and* a family. You must not only be passionate about what it is you want, you also need to take action to realize or actualize what it is you want.

Chances are you decided to become an entrepreneurial mom so that you would have the freedom and flexibility to work life and business around raising a family or the other way around. You may have become frustrated with trying to find someone else to care for your children and decided it would be easier to work for yourself and create your own hours. You probably learned very quickly that you need to maximize naptime to the fullest.

You may have become frustrated with the outside world dictating how you were going to live your life and decided it was time for you to have more control over your time and fulfilling your dreams and not someone else's. You may have become an entrepreneurial mom because you do not want to work for someone else, you don't like someone hovering over and watching your every move, and not having any autonomy or say in the outcome of a project. You may have also realized that you can build a business that not only supplements your family's income but can provide a substantial contribution to your family's bottom line.

There may be many other reasons that you became an entrepreneurial mom, but rest assured you can create a more balanced, happy, and fulfilling life in the process. You will need to roll up your sleeves and multitask and work harder and smarter than ever before. The entrepreneurial mom has the opportunity to provide the greatest impact in the world today.

The Dalai Lama once said, 'The world will be saved by the Western woman." More than that, I believe it is the entrepreneurial mom—the new woman of the twenty-first century—who will shift into conscious awareness of creating a life and a business she loves. This is not about juggling a career with family. It's about integrating various aspects of a woman's life to reach happiness, fulfillment, a life of freedom and flexibility to do what a mother wants to do for herself and her family—a life where she can profit and prosper and contribute to her family's bottom line. Women are nurturers who are the heart and glue of the family.

I am not claiming that my world is perfect. I am a mother who strives to find harmony and balance between growing my business, raising my family, and loving every minute of it. Challenges and roadblocks have come my way and I've learned ways to adapt and navigate my journey. I have interviewed many women, learning their definitions of success and what has worked and not worked in their businesses. I have read one to two books a month for over twenty years now. I have worked with business coaches to grow my business, and I set many goals and set targets which I strive to achieve on a daily basis. I have learned to be a coach to others, and also that I must be coached to learn and grow so I can share that knowledge with others.

I have had deep conversation with my spouse about my dreams and desires and what I believe I am capable of. I have learned that all a spouse or partner needs to know in the process is that they are an important part of the journey and you are still working on the goals for your family as well as your own. Love, appreciation, and living in gratitude make the world go 'round.

I welcome opportunities to learn and grow even if sometimes I make mistakes along the way. And believe me, they do happen. What you make of them all depends on if you choose to react or respond. I like to reflect on the situations that occurred in my day and how I could make them better so I can do better the next time. At the end of the day, if I help one person get one step closer to their goal I have succeeded. My mission is to make a difference by empowering women and helping them recognize their greatness so they can step into who they are meant to be.

Several years ago, I attended an eWomen Network luncheon where the founder, Sandra Yancey, read the audience *The Little Engine that Could*. I had not read the book in years. When asked to carry a heavy load across a mountain, many engines said they couldn't do it. When one little engine said, "I think I can." That engine was a girl! From that moment onward, my burning desire and the little voice inside me grew louder: I need to serve women in a big way. Just like the little engine, you can do amazing things in your business and life too! Yes you can!

The greatest mountains we face are the ones we create in our minds. Look a short distance in front of you and keep going. I like to refer to this as keeping the blinders on to prevent the distractions that come from comparing where you are to where others are. Every so often look back and see how far you have come versus focusing on how far you have yet to go.

This book is the entrepreneurial mom's guide for helping moms solidify their business identities, step into their greatness, strengthen their position in the marketplace, and learn the skills to survive the winds of change so they can step into the skin they were meant to be in. Your mindset, confidence, courage, marketing savvy, and relationship skills are the cornerstones of building a successful and rewarding business.

Every entrepreneurial mom can build a business and still serve the family she loves. If you're ready, let's begin!

With Gratitude, Debra Kasowski

Chapter 1

Becoming and Being—Knowing Who You Are and Owning It

"Success comes from knowing that you did your best to become the best that you are capable of." —**John Wooden**

Imagine: you come home from a meeting with a client and the house looks like a tornado hit it. Backpacks are strewn across the entryway, someone has left dirty dishes and glasses in the kitchen sink. You sit down and look at the heap of laundry waiting by the washer—and let out a big sigh. You have to get the kids off to their activities and your spouse is working late. You never thought working from home would make you feel like you were a juggler in a circus act. You have a business to run, a family to raise, and somewhere in there, you need to make time for you.

Your family obligations are overwhelming you and you simply cannot add more to your plate. The fleeting thought that it might just be easier to "get a job" and work for someone else enters your head.

But isn't that why you left the corporate world to begin with? You wanted the freedom to do what you wanted, when you wanted. You wanted the flexibility to look after your family on your own time and in your own way. You made the choice to create a life you love and not to have someone dictate your work hours to you or when you could take vacation. Now, you can go on the school fieldtrip, and then meet with a potential client and still be home in time for when the kids get home. You can be the mom and business woman you envision yourself to be—sometimes, it just seems overwhelming.

You made a choice—a choice to create a life you love—a life that cannot be defined by anyone else but you. The choices you have made have brought you to where you are today. It is in these times of doubt that you take a deep breath, dig deep, and remember why you're doing what you're doing, and the ultimate satisfaction you can bring to your life. You are an *entrepreneurial mom*!

Sounds like a superhero doesn't it? And indeed you are.

The term "entrepreneurial mom" describes a woman entrepreneur who runs her own business while managing the balance between her business and her family. She is often known as the queen of multitasking. Being an entrepreneurial mom is about taking action and getting things done. She has the drive to serve others more than she currently is—a calling, you could say, to serve the world in a bigger way.

An entrepreneurial mom is always evolving and growing into her passion. Each of us is on a journey to becoming and being our best selves. We are here to live our mission and our purpose. Best-selling author Richard Bach said, "Here is the test to find out whether or not your mission on earth is finished: 'If you are alive, it isn't.'" You have so much life to share.

Maybe you are at a place where you're feeling overwhelmed by your entrepreneurial life. Maybe you're just starting out: the kids have grown a bit, and you feel it's time to stretch your wings and focus more on what you want. Regardless of where you are, it's important to pause and review your values, your virtues, your passions to ensure that you're on the right track—that your business aligns with your inner life. Doing so will make those stressful days so much easier, as you will be more aware of the bigger picture, and reminded of why you do what you do, and that you're pursuing your purpose.

VALUES AND VIRTUES

Your values determine what is most important to you in your life. When you start making decisions that align with your values, you take full responsibility for your life and can more easily set boundaries with others. It can be challenging to find resolutions when others do not possess your same values. That is why in business you want to learn and understand what is important to the people you collaborate with or serve. What you value will become apparent in the way you market and live your personal brand. Your virtues reflect your core being and how you operate as a person. They are the standard by which you present yourself. Values and virtues work hand in hand with how you interact with people.

Following is a list of forty values. Take time to think about what each word means to you, then circle the seven values that are most important to you. It is also helpful to do this analysis by determining what is important to you as a family.

Accomplishment	Decisive	Motivator
Accountability	Disciplined	Optimistic
Advancement	Enthusiastic	Organized
Appreciation	Family-oriented	Passionate
Authentic	Flexible	Persistent
Being Fair	Good Communicator	Powerful
Being the Best	Happiness	Resilient
Bold	Hardworking	Resourceful
Caring	Humor	Truth
Celebrity	Inspirational	Variety
Challenged	Knowledgeable	Wealth
Collaboration	Leader	Wisdom
Competitive	Loyalty	
Confident	Marriage	

Now that you've determined seven values that are important to you, prioritize them. What are the top three most important values to you? Do you feel that these are the same three values people would use to describe you?

When you are able to identify and really define what your values are, you are acknowledging what is most important to you. Consequently, having a better awareness of your values and virtues will allow you to highlight these qualities in your daily life and your business life. Staying aware of your values will also help you make future decisions that align with what is most important to you.

> ### *Virtues are like the moral fiber that helps your operate in your life.*

I like to define virtues as the manner in which you display and bring your values into your environment. The people who you do business with and the people you interact with will be able to describe you and also know what you stand for. When your virtues and values are in alignment, people will know what to expect from you.

By adhering to your values and virtues, you choose to live by a certain code of honor. Consider it akin to organizations that have a written mission statement, vision, and values as part of their corporate identity that allows them to build a culture reflective of those statements. Virtues are like the moral fiber that helps your operate in your life.

Several years ago while I was still in the workplace, I gave out to coworkers rocks with different words inscribed on them like: Wisdom, Courage, Believe, and or Faith. The rocks were accompanied by notes that described why I felt the value inscribed on the rock applied to the particular person I presented it to. As I look back, I realize that for me, it was an exercise in saying: "I am paying attention to you and you matter." It ended up that it was a perfect way for someone to realize one of their values.

A month after I gave out the rocks, a staff member came up to me and asked me if she could give me a hug. She said, "You gave me a rock a month ago and I wanted to let you know you changed my life." I was a bit dumbfounded when she told me this as I had simply viewed the rock as an expression of for appreciation and gratitude for what these individuals already exuded. I admired them for the values and virtues they possessed and how they brought them to the workplace. I asked her what I had done. She told me that whenever she came to work, she placed the rock on her desk in front of her and focused on it throughout her day. Her rock was inscribed with the word *believe*. She went on to tell me that many things had been changing for the better as she had focused on believing in herself and her capabilities. I had simply been a conduit to remind her of a value she may have forgotten when times got tough.

Another staff member, James, told me that because of the rock with *faith* inscribed on it, he felt I would best be suited to give his daughter one of eighteen gifts at her eighteenth birthday party. Her party was like a debutante ball and was an amazing experience for all who attended. The birthday girl was dressed in a beautiful, bride like, white gown. Her friends had practiced a special waltz to dance for her on her special day. It was really like being in a fairy tale castle.

I was extremely excited to give my gift to the birthday girl. My inspiration for my gift came from Carrie Underwood's song "Remember Me." The song is about a mother who is helping her daughter pack up to go out into the world. The mother gives the girl a Bible, a map, and money in glove compartment of the car, so that her daughter will find her way home if she ever gets lost. That was what I gave James's daughter: a Bible and a map with that very message. Her parents gave her the key to their home so that she knew she was always welcome. This was a perfect example of how, when we inspire others, we also make it possible for them to share with us.

What I also did not realize until I reflected upon it, was that while I was working in alignment with what mattered to me, it also aligned with the people I was supporting.

Transparency is also a very good example of a virtue, and has been a buzz in the corporate world but also the entrepreneurial world. People want to know what is going on: no surprises, hidden costs, or hidden agendas. People are tired of feeling like they are being played, and they are getting clear about what they want their lives to look like, especially mothers like you nurturing our future generations.

When you are aware of your values and virtues, you can better connect with those around you and tap into what's important to them. I will expand more on this in Chapter Two. Being aware of your values and virtues can change the way you approach business presentations, conduct sales, and even operate as a family. We must examine our values, virtues and how we want to show up in the world so we can live, love, and matter.

Pursuit of Passion and Purpose—Getting in Touch with Your "Why"

> ## *Passion is the fuel that drives us to achieve our hopes and dreams.*

Passion is the fuel that drives us to achieve our hopes and dreams. As a mom, you're already in touch with your passionate side—even if you don't realize it. Think about how you felt at the birth of your first child. Think how you felt when you encouraged her in taking her first steps, or when he finally got potty training down. These moments were filled with passion, as you exalted in your children's success.

Take a moment and recall the time when you started your business. How excited were you? Did you want to tell everyone about what you were going to do? You may have had butterflies in your stomach and you may even have had trouble falling asleep at night because of your excitement. You may have felt ideas flooding in from all directions.

Now, however, you may feel that you have hit a plateau or that you've lost the focus you once had. If that's the case, it's perfectly understandable. Often, when all we have time to do is focus on the tasks at hand, or crossing off the to-dos on our lists, it can feel overwhelming and perhaps even routine. I find that during our craziest times we can learn how to strategically achieve what we need to get done. It is these times that you need to get laser focused on the results you want to achieve. If this is the case, you may need to reconnect with your *why*. *Why* did you choose to be an entrepreneurial mom? Why did you start the particular business you started?

Several years ago, I shared the stage with Janet Attwood, co-author of *The Passion Test: The Effortless Path to Discovering Your Destiny.* One insight she shared was that "to have absolute success in any area, the most important prerequisite must be that you have a passion for doing it." In my nursing career, I have witnessed the beginning of life by holding a newborn baby after their first cry, and I have also been there to hold someone's hand as they have taken their last breath. These moments have showed me the importance of living fully, in every minute—as each moment matters. You must inject passion into your life and business to live a life that is "rich from the inside out." Business, family, and life are not mutually exclusive! You want to fall in love with your business again and rejuvenate it so you can ignite the excitement you once had. Remember that no one can run your business with the love and attention you do.

So how do you regain that passion? You still feel passionate about your family and kids, so what's stopping you from infusing your passion into your business or yourself?

The best cure for boredom or hitting a plateau is tapping into your creativity to spark innovation. Here are some ideas: Take a new class or develop a new product or service in your business. The research you do and the learning curve will stimulate you. Read books or trade magazines that will give you new ideas and look for ways to implement what you learned into your business. But it's not just about rekindling your passion in your business. You also need to look after yourself on a more personal level. Recharge! Take some mommy time! Take that exercise class you've been thinking about but keep putting off. Schedule that afternoon lunch with the girls you've been meaning to have. When you make the time to reward yourself personally, your energy level rises and your enthusiasm grows. When you learn to infuse passion into your daily life, you will be more passionate when looking for ways to grow your business, and even become more creative in navigating raising your family while accomplishing some of your goals. You will be intentionally creating the life that you love because you will be doing *what* you love.

When you are passionate about your business, work, hobby, or interest, you have the desire to do it because you love it and it does not require effort. You are excited about it. You may even start your day a half hour earlier just because you want to, not because you have to. You chase your passion not to be paid for it, but because you love to do it. Passion is a way of life!

Passionate people are positive, enthusiastic, driven, and solution-focused. They find ways to express their passions and they persevere through the challenges that come their way as they envision their end goal. They seek out others who are like-minded and who share similar interests.

Living passionately is also contagious! Not only will you be a shining example of someone who is pursuing her dreams, but you will also allow others to pursue theirs as they will admire you for going after what you say you will. Have you ever noticed that many people are all talk and no action? Perhaps they are waiting for the perfect moment before they act. Guess what? There is no perfect moment. You create the right time and the right moment when you make a decision to go after what you want and start creating the life of your dreams.

As you build that passion into your daily life, also remind yourself of your *why*.

My Passion Pleasers

Take a few minutes to think about the following:
- What do I love to do?
- Does my business allow me to pursue this?
- What skill, talents, or abilities come naturally to me?
- Do I utilize these talents enough in my business? Do I use them at home with my family?
- When have I felt most fulfilled or happy?

While a woman pursues her passion and discovers her purpose, she may come to the conclusion that she is here to serve the world in a much bigger way—even bigger than she may have anticipated. When you come from a place of serving others with no expectation, you acknowledge and appreciate people for what they bring to the world. When people feel valued and you have helped them, they naturally want to reciprocate and assist you in achieving what you want and need. One of the greatest lessons I have learned is that when you are connected to your purpose (the *why* you are here) and your passion (the *why* you do what you do), your business will grow. People will share what you have done for them and the ripple effect will continue. The drive and determination that you have to get up every morning comes from being passionate about the life you know you were meant to live and living your purpose. Not only are you the heart of your family but the glue that keeps it together.

Discovering your "why" is so important. When you can connect back to your why, your whole world transforms and you become more passionate about how you live your life. Wouldn't it be great to wake up every day excited to start the day?

You are so much more than what you see in the mirror and you still have so much more to give and become. Too many women think that they need to be a certain size before they take action. Look around you! Success comes in all shapes and sizes. Knowledge varies to different degrees. The women who succeed get out of their own way and just take action! Know what is important to you in your business and how you are the solution in the marketplace to help others. You may be just the person someone is looking for, but if you are hiding and not letting anyone know how great you are, you cannot serve them.

Your vision and mission will give you a clue for your business. The hopes and dreams you have for yourself and your family are also part of your purpose as a mother.

Have you noticed a pattern yet? Your "why" has to do with people and making the world better than you found it. A children's book that is a favorite in our house, represents the importance of this perfectly. In Barbara Cooney's *Miss Rumphius*, a little girl listens to her grandfather's tales of his adventures at sea. She tells her grandfather that when she grows older, she too will go on many adventures like him, and then return to live by the sea. "That is all very well little Alice," said her grandfather, "but there is a third thing you must do." "What's that?" asked Alice. "You must do something to make the world more beautiful," said her grandfather. When Alice grows up, she does exactly that: she travels on many adventures and returns to live by the sea. She scatters many lupine seeds along the countryside to make the world around her more beautiful.

Just like Alice, you have the ability, through your business and with your family, to make the world more beautiful by going after your dreams and becoming the person you were meant to be. By following through on your passion and purpose, you not only are a beacon for others to do the same, but you make the world a better place because you have contributed your thoughts, your ideas, and opinions.

WHY-ercise

"If you don't know your why, you can't know your how." —**Simon Sinek**

You can complete this exercise on your own or with a trusted friend or colleague. Complete this exercise in a journal you can continue to write in and refer back to. Journaling is a useful tool to allow yourself to gather your thoughts and reflect. It is also a great tool for developing clarity and increasing your awareness. As you complete the exercise, allow yourself at least five minutes to reflect and focus on each area and question.

Your Business

- Why did you become an entrepreneurial mom?
- Why is your product or service important to the people you serve?
- Why do you want to be successful?

Your Family

- Why did you have a family?
- Why is being successful in your business important to you and your family?

Your Life

- Why do you want what you want?
- Why do you do what you do? For example, do you live in a certain area or drive a certain car for a reason? Think about how you do things. *Why* do you do it that way versus another way?

This reflective thinking helps you increase your awareness and acts as a spring board for investigating more questions about what's important to you, how to move forward, or how to let go of some of the things that may be holding you back. Once you are clear about why you are doing what you are doing, you will be more clear on your next action steps—the what and the how will also become more evident.

Here is an example of a few more questions that may come up:

- How will I feel when I live my *why?*
- How will I feel if I do not live my *why?*
- What can I do to follow my passion?
- How will others be impacted by my *why?*
- What is my contribution to the world?

In his book *Start with Why*, Simon Sinek states, "If you follow your WHY, then others will follow." When you see people following through on their hopes and dreams, they are a source of inspiration. This is one reason I love watching the Olympics. The athletes trained and sacrificed for their moment to give their best and win. As I see it, they were all winners because they knew their "why." All the sacrifices of missing parties or not eating that extra piece of chocolate cake are defined in one pinnacle moment that makes it all worth it.

As an entrepreneurial mom, you are like the athlete who tries to reach her personal best daily: getting the grass stains out of pant knees, refereeing sibling rivalry, making supper, potty training, all while compiling your new marketing campaign and maybe even getting to the gym. Connecting with your "why" will help you live your life passionately.

Becoming and being—realizing your values and connecting with your purpose— is all about being more aware of the decisions you make, the actions you take, and understanding that each little action and step is part of greater whole. You are constantly evolving into the woman, mother, and business owner you were meant to be. These roles are not mutually exclusive. They are one—they are *you* in one package.

I have been to many seminars and conferences and I have seen women sign up for programs, saying they bought different programs without knowing if they actually needed them. They spend thousands of dollars but do not necessarily implement what they have learned. You cannot just take these seminars or courses without taking some action so you can "become." Otherwise, the investment you make goes down the drain. It becomes "shelf help."

For every course you take, book you read, business or family decision you make, ask yourself: "Is this important to me? Is this decision in alignment with my "why"? Is this who I wish to become and be in the world?

Discover Your Strengths

The third element in becoming and being, as you blossom into the fullness of your potential, is to discover (or rediscover) your strengths. Having really focused on your values and purpose, you can really hone in on your strengths with great clarity and objectivity. It's also helpful to look back to past experiences and reflect on the times when others approached you for help or advice. What were they looking for from you? This could be a very good indication of where your strengths lie.

Most importantly, take a good look at yourself as a mom. Being a mother is one of the hardest and yet one of the most rewarding jobs in the world. As moms, we learn so many skills while running our households that we can transfer into the business world. We have gained our MBA in parenting and household management.

Take time to assess what you bring to the table in business and life. What do other people comment or compliment you on? Are you great at organizing events, planning schedules, or facilitating workshops? Discovering your strengths is the key to growing a business and life you love. When you are able to utilize the skills, talents, and abilities that come naturally to you, innovation and creativity will come easily and what some view as work will seem like play.

Completing the following SWOT (strengths, weaknesses, obstacles, and threats) analysis of yourself, your business, and your life will help you realize where you are excelling, where you may need assistance, and where you need to mobilize your resources to navigate or avoid potential obstacles or threats. The more strategic you can be in planning, the more successful and prepared you will be for any situation. By completing the SWOT analysis, you will position yourself with confidence and will be prepared to act courageously and take action based on due diligence.

ENTREPRENEURIAL MOM SWOT ANALYSIS

Read over, reflect, and answer the following questions as honestly as you can, remembering that there are no wrong answers. This is not a test that you can fail. The only time a woman fails is when she does not know what she wants. You can complete this exercise for yourself, your business, or the life you wish to create.

The Entrepreneurial Mom SWOT Analysis questions will help you identify what is working for you right now, and what you may need to spend more time, attention, and/or resources on. This exercise may also help you identify areas in which you may want to consider delegating to others who have a stronger expertise or interest in that particular area.

Strengths:

What do I do best?

What are my skills?

What are my talents?

What business knowledge do I possess?

If money were no object, what would I do for free? (What is something that I love so much it doesn't feel like work when I do it?) What makes me unique?

Weaknesses:

What do I struggle at doing?

What do I feel that I am not skilled or talented at?

Where do I lack knowledge and know someone could complete tasks more easily or efficiently than I?

Obstacles:

What is in the way of me obtaining my success?

Why do I think these things hold me back?

What can I do about it?

Threats:

What threatens my dream from coming true?

What can I do to protect or claim my dreams?

What would lessen the threat?

What have I done so far?

Breanne, forty-two and mother of two, owns an art gallery. Her SWOT Analysis looked like this:

Strengths:

What do I do best?

I'm good at building rapport and identifying unique artists to feature at the art gallery.

What skills do I possess?

Writing, budgeting, and setting up exhibitions.

What are my talents?

Coordinating exhibitions and writing press releases.

If money were no object, what would I do for free? (What is something that I love so much it doesn't feel like work when I do it?)

I'd sculpt, paint my own works. I love running my art gallery, but I would like to spend more time with my family.

What knowledge do I possess?

Master's degree in fine arts.

What makes me unique?
I am passionate about sharing art with the masses.

Weaknesses:

What do I struggle doing?
Marketing and sales, attracting new customers

What do I feel I am not skilled or talented at?
Web design, online marketing, and social media marketing.

Where do I lack knowledge and know someone could complete tasks more easily or efficiently than I?
Web and newsletter design. There are a number of people I could contact about this.

Obstacles:

What is the way of me obtaining my success?
Money, lack of staff, retention of artists

Why do I think these things hold me back?
Without more money, I don't think I can grow my business. I am afraid of what change would mean for my artists and for my business.

What can I do about it?
Discuss changes with my staff and artists. I can make changes by engaging the people affected.

Threats:

What threatens my dream from coming true?
Online art dealers, dealers who are selling art at lower prices.

What can I do to protect or claim my dream?
Start an online newsletter, showcase a new artist every month, and come up with an irresistible offer by working with my artists.

What would lessen the threat?

Developing a strong team with a similar vision. Attracting more clients. Get more involved in social media.

What have you done so far?

Hosted art exhibits, sent press releases that resulted in more media coverage.

Breanne found that the SWOT Analysis really helped her home in on what her next action steps should be. She may have been carrying many of these thoughts in her head, but putting them on paper made them more concrete and helped her to formulate an action plan.

Breanne hired an administrative virtual assistant to start an on-line newsletter, and she started featuring a new artist every month for her gallery. She made more time for her own creative outlet, and also began collaborating with artists to teach and showcase their skills to budding artists in the community. Students of the art lessons and patrons of the gallery started to rave about Breanne's work, which started attracting new clients to the gallery. She planned better in order to spend more time with her family. Breanne engaged her staff in her vision for the gallery and they in turn started to share their own vision as to how the gallery could grow.

The Entrepreneurial SWOT Analysis can help you identify what you need to do to grow your business.

Awaken the Confidence Within

One of our greatest obstacles, yet also our greatest opportunity, exists in our mind. I'm talking about confidence. A woman's confidence in herself and her abilities will always far exceed any deficit she may think she has. I am not speaking of arrogance or being too good for others, but a belief in one's self and faith that every effort she takes will help her reach her destination of choice.

Why not you; why not awaken the confidence within?

According to the Merriam-Webster online dictionary, confident is:

- a feeling or a consciousness of one's powers or reliance on one's circumstances
- what faith or belief that one will act in our right, proper, or active way
- the quality or state of being certain
- a relation of trust or intimacy

We demonstrate our confidence in many ways: how we carry ourselves, how we speak, and how we approach new situations.

Like all of us, you probably have areas in your life where you feel more confident than in others. It's possible that over the years you may have forgotten what it felt like to step out of your comfort zone and step into your potential of who you are meant to be. Take a moment to you think about your life as a mom.

Your child didn't come with a training manual. Do you remember when you brought your beautiful newborn home? You established a routine, but suddenly things went haywire. You may have read some parenting books, but overall you learned the business of motherhood as you went along, through trial and error. In business, you have access to many books and resources, but you will still have to learn by doing—by being confident in stepping outside your comfort zone. Motherhood taught you to adjust. It's the same with business: there's a great deal of trial and error and sometimes the way things once were are no longer. But these aren't reasons to not feel confident in your abilities.

Increasing your self-confidence can dramatically affect your performance. When you are more confident and have a positive self-image of yourself, you are open and welcome new opportunities that come your way. You increase your competency level, you are more productive and efficient, and you strengthen your team and your business. But most of all you will feel more confident to share your skills and talents and abilities and even your knowledge with other members of your community and with those you do business with. You become a glowing role model to other entrepreneurial moms who are climbing the ropes of their own success.

Our confidence develops over time as we increase our knowledge and competence level. Real-life experiences add to our competency and hence our confidence. Just like the phrase says: "Practice makes perfect."

Remember the time when your child awoke for the first time with a barky cough? You probably weren't very confident about what to do about your baby's croup. You might have panicked and called your mother or rushed to the emergency room. But the next time it happened, you knew you could take the baby outside, and let them breathe in some cool night air to reduce the inflammation in their airway. If that did not work, you knew you needed to go into the hospital. Each time and for each child, you learned better how to handle the situation. You were less reactive and more proactive in your approach.

You develop your business confidence in the same way. Life is a series of trials and errors in which we hope to succeed. With each trial, you learn to adjust so you can keep heading toward to the success you want. This confidence evolution occurs in business and life, simultaneously. You must also be aware of and make use of the resources you have around you. We all have resources around us but our success depends on how we utilize those resources.

Avoid Confidence Killers

Experiences and people from your past can have a great impact in your life today. Some can be wonderful influences, but others can be detrimental to your confidence level. They include teachers, coaches, heroes, grandparents, role models, mentors, and colleagues.

Jennifer, a mother of two, told me that she lacked confidence in her abilities to grow her business. In exploring why she felt this way, she recalled that she had a teacher who told her that she was stupid and would not amount to anything. Even as an adult, every time Jennifer would attempt to do something new, she could hear the teacher's voice in the back of her head, and eventually she would give up on the new endeavor. Once she realized the impact this memory was having on her, she worked on dismissing the teacher's opinion from her mind. As Jennifer's confidence grew her business did as well. She also found that the relationships with her family improved. She was better able to believe in her abilities and the greatness that was within her.

Denise, a mother of three, hired a business coach to help her grow her business and realize her potential in the process. Her coach was encouraging, even when Denise had moments of weakness and didn't believe in herself. With the help of her coach, Denise felt confidence in knowing that she was on the right track, and implementing ideas made her gain great strides in her business. She attracted more clients and started making more money.

These two examples show how people and the environment in which you are supported can directly affect your confidence. You must choose whose opinion you value and whether or not it is valid. Remember that there are over seven billion people in the world. Are you going to give one person's opinion that much power?

One of my greatest lessons came from a book called *The Four Agreements*, by Don Miguel Ruiz. Ruiz explains how a compliment or condemnation is just another person's opinion, and that we should not take them personally. Along these same lines, Eleanor Roosevelt said, "Nobody can make you feel inferior without your consent." You can choose whether or not to internalize another person's opinion. What really matters is the opinion you hold of yourself.

Comparing yourself to others can also be damaging to your confidence. This can even lead you to feeling that you're stuck in a rut, not making any traction. You can be making progress and moving forward, yet feel like you are not accomplishing anything. This happens because you have taken your eyes off the prize and steered off-course by comparing yourself to others. Let me make a confession: I have done it. Yes, I have compared myself to others only to lose my focus on what I truly wanted. It can be a vicious circle to get into.

Comparing yourself to others can easily start with admiration, but when you start saying things like "Oh, but look what she is doing" or "I will never be able to be that successful." Or even "She doesn't have kids, so she has the time." Do not fool yourself for one second, this is when you get caught in the comparison trap let's take a look at those phrases:

1. **"Oh, but look at what she is doing."** Look at what she is doing and think about the following because you can learn from it not just envy it. Whatever it is she focuses on she got the results for. ***Continue to focus on what you want and you will get the results you want or better—your way.*** You are also looking at one moment in time but not the sleepless nights and roadblocks or obstacles that she has faced. You may not want all the other things that came with the package.

2. **"I will never be able to be that successful."** First of all, define what success means to you. Success has many different meanings: money, happiness, having a family, creating warm memories, or personal fulfillment. You can be a success where you are by making the choice to be successful. What you believe, you will ultimately receive!

3. **"She doesn't have kids, so she has the time."** Kids or no kids, it comes down to basic time management and making your business has priority time and your family having priority time. There are many entrepreneurial moms out in the world making a difference. There are many mothers who are authors who get up early to write their books—one paragraph at a time. Drop the excuses. You can do it, your way!

When you compare yourself to others, you decrease the value of your self-. You may look at others and think their life looks so easy, their kids are so much better behaved than yours, or envy that they go on vacations twice a year. Sounds like the charmed life doesn't it? Do you know for sure that everything is a bed of roses? Every woman faces challenges in her life. Do not fool yourself. A wise woman once pointed out to me, "You look at their life for a moment, but live their entire life." I find that once you get to know people, they appear more vulnerable and no longer fit the ideal for which you propped them on a pedestal. You can see their life in a different perspective.

Confidence Leads to Success

As an amateur triathlete, I have learned that a triathlon is an excellent reference to life and business. Your success depends on your endurance. Can you transition quickly when circumstances arise? Can you hang in there for the long haul? Can you give your very best? Although competing in triathlons is about compete against others, it is primarily about competing against yourself and pushing yourself to achieve your personal best. Each time you compete, you try to do better than the last time you did it.

Just as you would if you were planning for a triathlon, you would set personal goals for yourself or for your business. Strive to stretch and better yourself every time you send an email, make a phone call, or do a presentation. Your success will come as your confidence grows. Each effort will compound over time to help you reach that destination.

And remember that the timing of your success and accomplishments will always show up at the right time for *you*. There may be a reason that you are still waiting for your defined success to arrive.

1. You have not clearly defined what success means to you so you do not know what it will look like for you. You could be already there.

2. The Universe or God is still aligning people, meetings, lessons, and circumstances to make everything fall into place.

3. You have not taken any action yet toward your goals and dreams. They are not going to fall into your lap or arrive in your mailbox. Remember you cannot win a lottery if you do not buy a ticket." You need to take action.

Shift Your Mindset

Your mindset and the voice that you hear playing in your head is one of the greatest obstacles that you need to overcome. You can get in your way of your success by talking yourself out of trying new things or out of doing the things you need to do to move forward in your business. The way you think about your talents, abilities, and skills has a great deal to do with the results you get. There are often words, phrases, or personal mantras that people say or think about themselves. Sometimes you may say things without even being conscious of them. The words you use have a great deal of power. Be careful what you say to yourself; you can be sabotaging your own efforts. Do you ever find yourself thinking one or more of the following statements?

- "I am not enough."
- "I do not deserve this."
- "I cannot do that."
- "I have nothing to share."
- "I do not have enough time."

> ## *Negativity has no place in your journey to success.*

Negativity has no place in your journey to success. So banish these statements from your life. You *are* enough. You deserve the best life has to offer. Why? Because you are worth it. Just be yourself. That's who the world is waiting for, and there is only one of you. You have plenty to share: your experiences help others, your knowledge helps others, and your skills, abilities, and talents help others—share them. You *can* set aside time for the things you really want. Growing your business has to do with changing habits and shifting your mindset to an "I can do" attitude. I am enough. I am worth it. I will make the time to do what is important to me. I can learn a new skill. I can start sharing my talents with others."

Your attitude plays an important part in how you respond and react to circumstances. By choosing not to let anything ruin your outlook on life and your business, you will be able to look at problems as possibilities, and obstacles and opportunities for growth. If you feel hit with the negativity bug, shift your thinking by reframing you statement in the positive and affirming your strengths.

Remember that a positive mindset can help you in a number of ways:

1. **It can keep you focused on opportunity and possibilities**, which leads to people wanting to be around you because you set an example of hope and possibility of a better life.

2. **It will allow you to take action** toward what it is you want to achieve. You do not need permission from anyone else. Each step you take creates momentum that motivates you to continue.

3. **It will allow you to learn from any mistakes you make, getting you** one step closer to learning what works and what doesn't. Redefine your strategy along the way. Look for the opportunities that lie within.

1. **It will allow you to develop an attitude of gratitude.** Your attitude towards life events and challenges is what inspires others. Be grateful for what makes your life great.

Are You Waiting to be Rescued?

Oprah once said, "One thing I know for sure is that we all want a better life." We are all trying to get ahead and trying to create that better life. But I see and hear so many people weighed down by excuses, expecting someone else to save or rescue them and take them to the life of their dreams. You know what? You are responsible for creating the life of your dreams. You cannot wait for others to pull through for you and create it for you. The other people in our lives do not necessarily have the same drive, commitment, and interest as we do for what we wish to achieve. They do not have the same hunger and desire you do for what you want.

If you want something bad enough, do what it takes to get it.

If you want something bad enough, do what it takes to get it. If you want your business to succeed, take a course, hire a coach, find the way to gain the knowledge or the resources you need to get what you want. Utilize resources from your local library, open the conversation with people who have done what you want to do, and check out social media platforms like You Tube and blogs about your topic.

If you were stranded on a deserted island, would you find a way to build a fire to signal someone for help? Or would you just kick back and suntan, hoping someone will notice you are missing? What are the chances you will be rescued in these scenarios? Your business works the same way.

When I wanted to hire a business coach, I had other expenses I need to pay off. However, I knew that the money I invested in coaching would help me grow my business to generate more income. My solution was to work shifts as a nurse to make the money I needed to pay for my coach and my expenses. I've know many people who get a part-time or temporary job to fulfill this type of need. One woman I know took a temporary position making phone calls for a car dealership regarding the latest promotions or courtesy calls post purchase. As a mom, you could babysit or temporarily help others with before- or after-care. Do not put yourself down for choosing to get ahead while looking after your family. There is more than one way to get to the same destination.

Be resourceful! You can come up with ways to make things happen. Review the resources you already have. Tap into some of your skills that can make you the money you need in order to get what you want. When you work for it, you are more likely to implement what you have learned because you have made an investment of time, money, and resources.

After all, if your child needed winter boots or food, and you did not have the money, what would you do? Would you sit around waiting for the lottery to strike or would you get a part-time job of some type to look after your family?

If you want things to change, you must change.

It's important to realize that there are times when we need to put our pride on the backburner to understand the lessons we can gain from being in a less than ideal situation. Your biggest learning may be that you never want to feel like this again, or you may learn new skills and conquer some fears in the process. If you want things to change, you must change. This is part of my "no nonsense policy." What are you going to do about it? I ask myself this anytime I feel stuck. Not to be harsh, but sometimes we need to give ourselves an extra push to make some changes.

What Does It Mean When An Entrepreneur Says "I Do"?

Do you like being your own boss? Do you love nurturing your ideas and watching them grow? Are you eager to see the results of your efforts? If you answered yes to these questions you must be an entrepreneur! Entrepreneurs are unique as they:

- thrive and get a thrill from watching their ideas grow and prosper
- are innovators
- are creative
- love to be their own boss and call the shots
- love the freedom and flexibility of the lifestyle
- are hardworking
- are willing to sacrifice
- are risk takers
- can see the big picture or vision

- are persistent and resilient
- enjoy a challenge
- discover solutions to problems

What really makes them different from everyone else? It is their drive and commitment that set them apart from all the rest. Entrepreneurs work long and hard to achieve the results they want, and they are strategic in how they use their resources. Every action you take counts! They make a commitment to themselves and say, "I do!" If you are an entrepreneur, raise your right hand and repeat after me:

The Entrepreneur's Creed

I believe I became a business owner to make a difference in people's lives by being the solution and not the problem.

I will not give up when the going gets tough.

I will rise to challenges and even seek them out if necessary.

I shall do my due diligence with every deal.

I will learn from my mistakes, and may others forgive me if I have wronged them.

I am here to serve first and help people in the process.

I will share my talents, skills, and abilities with others.

I will give back to my community and leave a legacy I wish to be remembered for.

I will know my worth and charge for it. After all, I am an entrepreneur. This is how I make a living.

I will look my fears in the face and use them to my advantage.

I must set my agenda around my lifestyle and aim to create balance.

I will ask for help and guidance along the journey. I will focus on my goals and the direction I wish to head.

I will lead the way and help others climb to their highest potential.

I will not compare myself to others. I am unique and no one can do it my way!

I shall look for the possibilities and opportunities in every challenge.

I will stay motivated by celebrating my wins as I live my passion.

I will step out of my comfort zone on a regular basis. As I stretch, I will grow into the person I have yet to be.

I have a voice, and will share my message with the world.

I will take full responsibility for my actions and commit to being my very best each day.

Above all, I will remember the "why" I became a business owner. I believe I became a business owner to make a difference!

> *There is nothing more powerful than being around a woman who knows what she wants and goes after it.*

There is nothing more powerful than being around a woman who knows what she wants and goes after it. She is unstoppable. Confidence radiates around her and she attracts the success she wants—creating the life she loves and prospering. An entrepreneurial mom is clear on what she wants, lives by her values, developed her strengths, makes thoughtful decisions, and channels her confidence into being an action taker.

Get out there and let others know what you do. Your confidence is magnetic. People will want to know your secrets to success. Action takers get noticed and often look like overnight successes! You may be the next one!

Chapter 2

You Had Me at "Hello"
—Communication and Presentation

"Take advantage of every opportunity to practice your communication skills so that when important occasions arise, you will have the gift, the style, the sharpness, the clarity, and the emotions to affect other people." —**Jim Rohn**

We all remember the scene in *Jerry MacGuire*, when Dorothy (Rene Zelleweger) says to Jerry (Tom Cruise), "You had me at hello." Tom Cruise's character had just expressed his undying love for Dorothy in an impassioned, long-winded avowal of love.

Sure, it would be great to be able to walk into a room and grab the attention of others like Tom Cruise did in the movie. But in the real world, we also need people to remember us past the *hello*. The way we present ourselves and the way we communicate are of paramount importance to our businesses.

You took a big leap when you entered the entrepreneurial world. Word of mouth marketing and sharing your passion about your business is going to determine whether your business will succeed or fail. When you know your strengths, values, and purpose, have confidence in yourself, and face every day with a positive mindset, you can create and see opportunities and possibilities all around you. You also have a story that people can learn from, relate to, and appreciate. You must speak with confidence and conviction so others will believe in your business and see the advantages or benefits it offers them. Whether you are speaking to an individual or to a group, you need to move from connection to conversation by building trust. Your conversations matter.

Have you ever been at a networking event when a woman walks into the room and everyone looks up as she makes a grand entrance? Have you ever been at coffee shop and overheard two women having a conversation you found intriguing? If you said yes, would you like to be that woman? You can be!

Your Voice Needs to Be Heard

Several years ago, I was attending a speaking course and one of the sessions was conducted by Arthur Samuel Joseph of Vocal Awareness. He has worked with many actors, actresses, speakers, and even NFL players to help them ensure that their messages are conveyed in a manner that people will be sure to listen. Arthur Samuel Joseph is passionate about coaching people to stand in their power and appreciate the gifts they are given through their voice and message.

Until I attended his session, I had never really thought about how important our voice is when sharing a message. The session taught me that the way we speak and project our voice allows us to stand in our power, if done correctly. During that session, I witnessed many transformations after participants focused on their voice.

Janice, a petite young woman, was asked to stand up and share her name and little bit about herself. She was very shy and glanced down at the floor. Arthur asked her to simply raise her chin, take a kind loving breath, and to be thankful for her gifts before she spoke. With these simple changes in attitude and stance, when Janice spoke again, her sweet voice carried throughout the room, the audience yearned to hear more from her, and a huge applause broke out. I was amazed.

If no one knows your story, you cannot change the world.

> ## *If no one knows your story, you cannot change the world.*

There are many women like Janice who have so much to share with other women around them but they are frightened to be heard. Often, this fear stems from childhood experiences when they were told not to share their voice. Remember the saying, "Children should be seen, not heard"? If you do not share your voice, no one will know your story. If no one knows your story, you cannot change the world.

You need to learn to stand in your power and own who you are by believing in the gifts you bring to the world. When you believe in those gifts, skills, talents, and abilities so will the people around you. You will also show up as being a confident woman, a woman and a mom who means business. People will begin to take you more seriously as a business owner versus a hobby owner. Hobbies are for interest sake whereas businesses are formed to make money and grow.

Communication Tools

Communication can be both verbal and nonverbal. Following are some simple yet crucial nonverbal communication tools that will aid when speaking with others—both in business and your personal life. They may seem like obvious items, but it's amazing how often people fail to follow them. Personally, I am a "people watcher." One of my favorite places to watch people interact is in a shopping mall or at a food court. You can learn a lot about people by observing their interactions with others. The next time you're out, take time to observe how other people interact with one another. You'll be surprised at how much you can learn.

Remember, life and business are about people and relationships. Communication is what makes the bond stronger.

Smile

Your greatest accessory is your smile. Your whole personality lights up with a simple smile. Smiling shows you are inviting, friendly, and approachable. Practice smiling even when you are talking on the phone. A smile adds to your energy and excitement about what you do. I recently phoned a grocery store and asked to speak to the manager. The woman who answered on the other end exuded happiness and a huge smile that I could only imagine. When I commented on her behavior to her manager, she stated that this woman was like this daily and that her smile brought joy to all the people who encountered her. Wouldn't it be great to surround yourself with people like this?

Handshake

There are no secret handshakes in business or in networking, but your handshake might tell a few secrets about you. A limp handshake is characteristic of someone who lacks confidence or interest in the person with whom they are shaking hands. An overly strong handshake may indicate nervousness or arrogance. A handshake that means business is one that connects in the crease of the thumb on both hands and is firm.

Eye Contact and Body Language

Experts say that 50 to 70 percent of what is communicated is communicated through nonverbal communication. You cannot base your conclusions about a person's communication by a single factor such as a head nod or crossed arms. You need to look at clusters or patterns in their behavior.

Your facial expressions, eye contact, your physical stance, and your posture can communicate even more than the words being said during a conversation. You are communicating even when you are not speaking. People can pick up on your emotions and attitude by the look on your face or how your body is positioned. Your facial expression can convey happiness, sadness, excitement, confusion, anger, fear, and surprise.

You have probably heard the saying that the "eyes are the window to the soul." You can gather a great deal of information from a person's eyes. Eye contact can show interest or disinterest in a conversation.

In North America, making eye contact is the way to gain your listeners' attention, engage your audiences, and project openness. If you avoid eye contact, people may assume you are hiding something or avoiding being truthful. (In some cultures, however, avoiding direct eye contact is a sign of respect.)

If you are speaking in a group of more than two people, make eye contact with one person for one to three seconds, and then shift your attention to another person, eventually including everyone in the group. This will ensure that no one feels ignored or uncomfortable.

When you are presenting or in conversation, pay attention to a person's body language. Crossed arms may indicate defensiveness or closed off, however, look at clusters of information such as a person's facial expression or eyes. They may be relaxed or feel that the room is cold. Crossed legs may also indicate being closed off or a way to position one's self away from another. Tapping, fidgeting, or playing with a smart phone may indicate boredom or impatience.

A person's posture can also tell us about their personality and how confident they are about themselves and what they represent. After all, you are your brand remember. You want to be able to stand tall with your shoulder back and walk with confidence. You will be communicating that you are approachable and friendly. When you are seated at a table, you want to lean a bit forward to demonstrate interest into the conversation. Your body language can say more than your words do.

Facial Expressions

Your facial expressions can express many different emotions. Ensure that your facial expression is congruent with your message. If you are speaking about something sad, do not smile at the same time as you are sharing the story.

If a person is biting their lip, they may be worried about something or in deep thought. A person with pursed lips may be disappointed or displaying disapproval.

Your Tone of Voice, The Power of the Pause, and Silence

Your tone of voice is a powerful tool in communicating your message. Your tone of voice can express confidence, warmth, and approachability. You can leverage your voice and communication style in a way that heightens interest, shows enthusiasm, and engages the people you are speaking to. Have you ever spoken with someone or listened to a speaker that was monotone? I remember many years ago watching *The Glass Menagerie* with John Malkovich and explaining to my English teacher how painful it was for me to watch the movie. The character was so monotone, I began to lose interest.

Your tone of voice also indicates whether you are making a statement or asking a question. When you ask a question, your voice tends to naturally go up at the end. When you make a statement the tone is fairly even. However, if your tone goes up at the end of a statement, you may confuse the person you are speaking to as they will not know if you are asking a question or trying to make a statement.

Pauses are another very powerful way to communicate your message. This technique is powerful when you are making an important point before continuing to speak. Silence works similar to the pause. You may have shared a story relating to the person you are talking to or asked a question. Sometimes people need a moment to process what you have just said and what it means to them. This is the difference between feeling sold to or deciding on the sale. People need to digest what is being said.

Why Speaking in Business Matters

Public speaking or speaking to a group of people has been said to be one of the greatest fears people have, other than that of death. Would you believe that one of your greatest fears can be your greatest asset? You might say, "I can speak to people individually but really start getting uncomfortable in groups bigger than five or six people. Then I feel like all the attention is on me." Well, it is! You are part of a "show" where you need to show and tell people about what it is you do. In the entrepreneurial world word-of-mouth marketing and how you speak with people can be used to your advantage if you can create an experience that people want to be a part of. You need to learn to harness your fears and to speak with confidence and conviction for others to believe in your business and your message. People need to feel and understand what is in it for them.

The art of communicating in sales has much to do with the art of storytelling. When you tell a story—something that is not just based on facts and figures—you move people to action based on the emotional experience they have had with you. You take the sales out of selling as you are come from a place of helping someone acquire or reach a certain goal. In storytelling, you find a common ground and relate to your potential and existing customers through a story of someone in a similar situation and the results they had. You can make them the heroine of the story. Sometimes, you may need to pull out the fact and figures if that is what you client wants, but make sure you tie them into your story. By understanding what is important to them and what they are trying to achieve, you can use a story to illustrate an outcome they wish to achieve. Real life stories are so powerful in not only telling a story but teaching to fulfill a need.

> ***The more passionate you are about your topic, the more you can evoke emotion and connection with others.***

Even if you do not wish to become a professional speaker, the way you communicate with others has a direct impact on the way you do business and speak with others in small groups and one on one. Communication is an everyday part of life. Your communication style will determine how you connect with colleagues, customers, friends, and family. If you attend a tradeshow, you will be meeting many strangers. You need to get out from behind the table and engage your audience. You want to show confidence when engaging with people and telling them why you do what you do and what's in it for them. You will be able to handle any sales objections as you can relate to the pain and provide a solution. The more passionate you are about your topic, the more you can evoke emotion and connection with others.

Prepare a script for yourself if tend to get nervous. Practice in front of your family or the mirror to see how you carry yourself and maintain eye contact. The more you practice, the less nervous you will become and the more natural you will be as you speak with others. Eventually, with practice, you will no longer need the script. Before you know it, you may be teaching what you know about communication to others.

Toastmasters International

Toastmasters International is an organization that helps people develop confidence in public speaking, but it can also be beneficial just to improve your speaking abilities. The program helps you develop speeches and presentations, structure your content, and build stories that engage your audience. There are many toastmasters groups across the nation, and probably one in your community. You can learn more about this organization at www.toastmasters.org.

Speaking Associations

You may learn to love public speaking so much that you find you can create a revenue stream or build a profile of your products and services through speaking. In the United States the speaking association is called the National Speaking association (NSA), www.nsaspeaker. org. In Canada, the speaking association is called the Canadian Association of Professional Speakers (CAPS), www.canadianspeakers.org. Meeting planners and conference organizations search these websites to find speakers that will best fit their themes or audience's needs.

How to Gain Control Over Your Fears

I believe each one of us has some type of fear that we would like to work toward overcoming. I do not know anyone who would prefer to live in fear. Some people try to hide from their fears, whereas others tiptoe around them. Fear is often a case of feeling a lack of control over a situation.

A couple of years ago, I challenged myself to try something called the West Coast Slide. It's a track with a sled that has a joystick for accelerating or braking. Because I'm not a big fan of speed, I thought this might be a good way to try and face my fear a little. The whole slide time took under thirty seconds. And at the end of it I was exhilarated. The attendant noted that I hadn't been scared because I had control! How very true. Your fears dissipate when you feel that you have control.

The following are four ways to that you can gain control over your fears of communicating with others. (You can also think about other areas in your life where you would like to feel that you are more control and apply these methods there as well.)

- **Remember to breathe and make eye contact.** When we are afraid, we may hyperventilate, gasp for air, or hold our breath. Keep in mind my favorite sayings, "If you always remember to breathe, everything will be fine." Breathing smoothly and evenly is essential. It helps you pace your words and keep you calm.

- **Know your content.** Whether you are preparing for a one-on-one meeting or for a presentation, make sure you know your subject matter or about the company or person you are meeting with. Not only will it show that you took interest, it will also help you relate to the person or people you are speaking with. Do some research into who you will be presenting to, what their wants, needs, and fears may be. When you know this information, you can create a plan to address and help others overcome their obstacles. You know your expertise and know more than the people you are presenting to. No one can communicate *you* better than you.

- **Practice, practice, practice.** The more prepared you are for what you want to do, the more natural it will feel. You will be able to go through the motions with confidence and get the results that you want.

- **Mind over matter.** Many of the fears we have are perceived and probably will never realize. Sometimes, you just need to ask yourself: "What is the worst thing that could happen? How likely is it that this could occur? Do I know 100 percent that what I fear will come true?" Chances are you do not know. Prepare your mind for victory. Shift your mindset by asking yourself: "What will it feel like to conquer that fear and achieve what I want?"

  Every time I get up on stage to give a speech, I felt a small twinge of fear and excitement bundled in one. I take a deep breath and tell myself, "I got this. And I'm grateful to be sharing my message." Remember, people know what it takes to get on a stage or make a presentation. They appreciate you sharing your message. In the majority of cases, they are glad it is you and not them. If you engage your audience and make them part of your story, they will be busy listening and focused on you and your message. Channel your energy into your message— let the people listen to you and feel your presence.

- **Be Yourself.** Authenticity, vulnerability, and honesty make you human and someone people can relate to. Chances are the person or people you are speaking with are glad you are the one on the stage instead of them.

The more at ease you are speaking about your business, the more clients you will attract and engage with, and the more money you will make. People will sense your energy and passion and will want to learn more.

Presentation—Say It with Style and Grace

We've all heard the phrase, "Do not judge a book by its cover." Yet, we also know that most of us do anyhow. It has taken me time to learn not to make judgments before getting to know a person fully. I was once at a movie launch, and watched a woman walk across the room. I looked at her and thought to myself that her clothes were tacky and that she was wearing too much makeup. Little did I know, she ended up being the guest speaker and actually spoke about judging others before getting to know them. As she spoke about herself and her accomplishments, I could feel myself sliding down in my seat in shame and embarrassment. Ugh! It is human nature for us to look at others and compare yet it can be to our detriment. I learned from that day that until you get to know a person and where they have come from, you cannot make a judgment. People can surprise you. She shared her incredible journey and many lessons that we all could learn from.

So, although we should all work on not judging people at first glance, let's remember that most people do this. First impressions make quite an imprint on our minds.

Dress for Your Success

How you dress every day does matter. How you dress also communicates how you feel about yourself and your personality also shines through. It's not just important to dress for success when we're in public, it's also important to note that how you dress can also affect your performance even when you sit behind your computer. Think about it. Do you perform differently talking on the phone in pajamas versus office attire?

How you dress communicates how you feel about yourself.

You are not always going to be behind the safety net of your computer. People do business more readily with people they know, like, and trust. People are more trusting when they meet you in person than just a single interaction online. You're going to have to get out there to attend networking events, seminars, and conferences. You need to. You do not want to look like you just rolled out of bed. Here is a surprise for you. The person you see yourself to be is how others will also see you. How do you want to be seen? The way you care about yourself is a direct reflection of how much care and attention you will give your customers.

As moms, many of us toss our hair in a ponytail, pull on a T-shirt and a pair of capris, and go out with the kids. Let's be honest, some moms tend to let go of their appearance all together, as they have been putting themselves last. For some, this translates into how they dress for business.

You are your own marketing tool, a walking billboard of the business and person you represent. You are your brand. When you think of a brand you may think of Pepsi or Coke? Your brand is what you want people to remember you for. Branding is the words and phrases you and others use to describe you. You may review your strengths again to identify key descriptors of your brand. It is important that your appearance portray a message of confidence and credibility that is aligned with who you are.

You want the clothing you wear to fit you and the colors to flatter you. Choose pieces you can mix and match to create a variety of outfits. They do not have to be expensive pieces to look great. One of my most complimented outfits is a red suit I bought at thrift store for $7.99 while looking for Halloween costumes for my kids. You can be thrifty and discover some great finds. I have also discovered high-end consignment shops and other retailers that have helped create the look I am looking for. You may have even seen celebrities' outfits and their cost in one side of a magazine page and then on the other how you can create the same look for less. Really, who is going to pull back your collar and look at who made your outfit? What matters is how you wear it!

A great starter wardrobe may include:
- two pairs of pants (black, grey, navy, or brown)
- two skirts (black, grey, navy, or brown)
- two blouses or two camisoles
- one suit jacket or pant/dress suit
- cardigan
- black pumps
- Accessories (earrings, necklaces, broaches, or scarves can really change a look and create variety.)

Take a look in the mirror or take a picture of how you look in your outfits. You need to love how you look when you look in the mirror. Would you do business with you?

Create a Polished Look

An easy way for a woman to create a polished look is to have well-manicured hands, shaped eyebrows—as they were the frame of the windows to the soul—and a great haircut.

Find a contemporary hair style that suits the shape of your face and one that is easy for you to style on your own in a few minutes—especially if you need to tend to the kids in the morning. If you color your hair, make sure to get your roots done between coloring, if necessary. I have even discovered a special type of hairspray that helps me cover up some of those roots in between colorings.

Too much makeup can make you look as though you're in costume. Keep you makeup natural unless you are going on camera or video. Use a foundation to even out your skin tone, a neutral eye shadow, mascara to draw attention to your beautiful eyes, and lipstick or lip gloss will help finish off a very natural look.

Putting It All Together: Intentional Networking—We Are Not Playing Blackjack

Networking is a business-social activity when people gather together to mix and mingle in the hopes of meeting someone they may synergistically be attracted to in order to do business together or gain referrals.

Traditionally, networking is about people giving their thirty second "elevator pitch" where they say their name, their business, and the basics of what they do. When you go to events with structured networking, how many times do you want to hear the same elevator pitch? Personally, I am not a big fan of the elevator pitch; however, I do think it is useful when gaining clarity about your message. At The Millionaire Woman Club, instead of using the elevator pitch, I facilitate thought provoking questions related to our speaker's topic. This method helps focus our attendees on the speaker but also helps women get to know each other on a personal level and build the "know, like, and trust" factor.

Although first impressions are made in a matter of these first thirty seconds, it takes a bit longer to build rapport and a relationship in which a potential customer or business colleague gets to know, like, and trust you. In fact, it is said that it can take seven to nine "touches" or encounters before someone will do business with you.

I remember a networking meeting where a number of women were gathered, chatting, and learning about each other, when Denise, new to the networking world, went up to each person interrupting the conversation saying, "Here you need my card!" She then handed her card out to all the women in the group and then proceeded to the next group.

You can imagine what happened to her cards. Many of the women dropped them into the nearest garbage can. Denise had made no emotional connection. She didn't create the "know, like, and trust" factor.

Networking is not about collecting the most cards. Networking is about creating connections at an emotional level where people want to do business with you because they've gotten to know you, like you, and eventually trust you.

When you go to a networking event, tradeshow, or social event, you are going with the *intention* to meet someone, build a relationship, and potentially introduce them to your business. So when you go to an event, don't stand there like a deer caught in the headlights. Go and introduce yourself. Of course this can be intimidating if you are not used to doing so, but the more you step out of your comfort zone, you'll be amazed by the connections and referrals that you will actually have.

When you meet people at a networking event, try follow-up with them via e-mail, a phone call, or a meeting in order to continue to build that relationship with 24-48 hours after the event. This is not a one-time occasion. It takes time to build rapport, build trust, and share your mission vision and values. This is why it is so important to live your personal brand. Successful business owners know that the more relationships you can build the greater your network and net worth will be.

Tips for Intentional Networking

Go with an intention. How many people do you want to meet? What type of people do you want to connect with? When you are in conversation, there is nothing wrong with communicating with others the type of people you are looking to connect with. Aim for three to five people, otherwise you may not be able to nurture the relationship or learn how you can best serve them. Maybe the person you are speaking with will know of someone and refer you to them. You never know where your connections will be. Who does someone else know that needs to know you?

Act as if everyone in the room is someone you know. When you go into a room with confidence and fearlessness, you will be more comfortable with introducing yourself to others.

Whenever I have a speaking engagement, I arrive early to ensure that the room is set-up the way I need and that I have time to introduce myself to some of the people in the audience. By doing this, I am already creating a connection with the people who I will be speaking with. Sometimes I even have the opportunity to ask a few individual questions about some of their challenges to ensure I can address some of their concerns in my talk, making the connection deeper.

Always have your business cards with you. Your business card should be on nice, heavy cardstock. This is one tool that you do not want to cheap out on if you can; after all it's often what people have to remember you by. There are several online companies like *www.vistaprint.com* where you can get cards made at a reasonable price.

When designing your card, look at what you like and dislike about other cards you have received. Many business cards have the all or some of the following information:

- Picture or a logo, or both
- Mission Statement
- Title
- Phone/Cell/Fax
- Email Address
- Mailing Address

Your business card is like a fine piece of real estate. Use it wisely – both front and back. *Have a call to action!* You may even pose couple questions about potential challenges that make the receiver of the card think about how you may help them or someone else they know.

Conversations into Connections—Creating Relationships that Matter

Have you ever wondered how you take that great conversation you had with someone and turned it into a meaningful connection that could lead to friendship, collaboration, and of course new prospects. Once you have had the conversation, it is time to build rock solid connections-relationships in business that matter. It's about getting to know people for who they are not just what they do or have.

Focus on being fully present with whomever you are speaking. This gesture makes what they are saying valued and makes them feel that they matter.

Sylvia, thirty-five and a mother of two, took time to reflect on what she wanted people to say about her. She explained that she had been described as flighty and distracted. These comments really bothered her as she wanted to be known as someone who was present and focused in the moment. In order to do this, she made sure that whenever she had a conversation with someone; she made eye contact and actively listened to the person, paraphrasing back to them what they had said. Not only did Sylvia become more present in the moment, but this simple change transformed her business because she was better able to ask questions that mattered to the people she was in contact with. She made people feel important, valued, and appreciated. The change she made did not cost her any money but she definitely made some.

Be Interactive and Involved

Volunteering in the community shows that you care about giving back. Engaging with others in the community can also increase your business's profile. You will be seen as a "giver."

Gail, forty-four and mother of two teenagers, was shy and had few close friends. She never went to networking groups. She basically hid behind her computer and her online business. But she yearned to take risks, help others, and contribute to the community. I encouraged her to volunteer in her community and while doing so, to be prepared to answer the question, "What do you do?"

Gail volunteered in various capacities with her children's activities, served food at a homeless shelter, and joined the board of advisors for community development. While she was doing this, she met amazing people who learned about her children, her passion for online marketing online, and her giving spirit. She shared her story and her passions. People started to hire her and refer her to others.

Within six months of volunteering and attending one networking meeting a month, she began to glow as she started conversations and got excited about her life and her business. Her children commented how much more fun who she was to be around and how much more they wanted to do things with her in the community.

There are several keys to success in business. However some of these keys will be higher priority than others because you don't want to come across as the slimy, slicked-back hair sales person from the movies. The people who you serve want to know what is in it for them. You need to be an active listener. You need to take time to listen not only to the words being said but pay attention to what your customer needs are. Take time to listen to the people you have the conversations with, because they matter. One of my biggest life and business turnarounds came from a quote I found by Leo Buscaglia: "Too often we underestimate the power of touch, a smile, a kind word, a listening ear, and honest compliment, or the smallest act of caring, all which have the potential to turn a life around." It's about making it about the people. And people are why you are in business.

Develop your curiosity by learning from your children and asking questions. Think about a time when you responded to one of your children's questions, and they continued to ask you "But why?" You would respond, and they would continue to ask you "Why?" The pattern would continue for several minutes until you just announced: "Because!" You need to learn and discover what your prospect or your customers *why* is. Find out what's important to them by getting to know what their end goal is. What product or service might they need for their business, and how might you be the solution that can support them. One of the most important things is to find a common interest and how can you relate to this person on the human level. Do you both have kids or enjoy a similar sport? You have heard of six degrees of separation. Learn about where people grew up, went to school, where their children go to school. You never know who knows someone you know. When you discover how you can relate to someone on a personal level and get to know a person for who they are, you can be of better service to them. This is one of the ways that you take a person from being an acquaintance or conversation to ultimately a connection and a potential referral.

Can you see the difference between imagining the slimy salesperson and someone who just cares about helping you lead a better life? Who would you want to do business with?

Success is built by people; nurture others.

Most of all, align with like-minded people. These are the people who support you and help you grow your business and even help you raise your family. You cannot do it alone, and neither can they. We are meant to collaborate and support one another in getting to our end goals. Success is something that is built by people, not in silos.

When you meet people and grow your network, think about whom you need to follow up with in order to make a difference. The biggest thing is your *follow-up*! Are you going to follow-up with a phone call or an email? Did you get permission to send them your e-zine or newsletter so you can connect with them to continue that relationship? Whether it is through email, phone calls, or in person, you want to continue to nurture the relationships around you.

Keep Track of Who You Know

Build a spreadsheet or maintain a database of the people you connect with, and keep track of the last you've met, your common interests, and their interests. If you know that they love to cook for their families, you might send them a note to say that you are thinking of them and send them a new recipe or a cookbook. Perhaps you are having a conversation about fashion, and came across that great store or you saw magazine article, you may want to just call them up and let them know that you are thinking of them once again or send them the article.

At an eWomen network event, I learned about "Fortune is in the Follow-Up" (FIITFU) prospect/client database, which can be extremely useful in helping you keep up with your network. The program not only allows you to store all your contacts but it also has reminder capabilities to ensure you consistently and regularly follow up with the people in your networking circle.

Chapter Two

The Other Side of Communicating — Asking For What *You* Want

In communicating with others, it's also important to voice who you are and what you want or need. Some people think that asking for help is a weakness, but it actually can be your greatest strength. Some people are afraid to ask for help because they feel vulnerable and weak. They feel that they should be able to look after themselves without the help of others. This is a martyr attitude that can easily turn into resentment because they are left doing all the work.

Others might fear that if they get a positive response to their questions, they may actually have created work for themselves. Still others fear looking stupid when they ask questions, not realizing that there are other people probably thinking or wanting to ask the same thing. No question is a dumb question. Questions are the answer to what we need to do next.

Women who ask for what they want are very powerful and confident. These women can look at a situation and ask for what they want in such a way that they create a win-win situation that supports the business or community they are working with. Asking is not a transaction. It is part of building a relationship and supporting others. Having a natural curiosity about the world around you can give you better insight as to how you can help others on their journey.

> *Asking for what you want not only helps you get what you want helps others ask for what they want.*

Zig Ziglar once said, "If you can dream it, then you can achieve it. You will get all you want in life if you help enough other people get what they want." People naturally like to help people succeed. I have found that when you ask people to help support you, you actually get more support than you may have ever imagined. Asking not only helps you get what you want but it also helps others to ask for what they want.

Asking for something for yourself is kind of like being at high school dance. You can sit along the wall of the gym, waiting for someone to come and ask you to dance. Then, when the cute boy has asked you, you may feel uncomfortable as you reluctantly reach out toward him. The first steps of the dance may seem awkward, but slowly you develop a rhythm. The dance is light and you are swept off your feet. Why? Because others around you have supported you, all because you got up and met opportunity instead of just sitting around.

I use this analogy because I have seen time after time, myself included, where we have an opportunity to ask for help and we don't. We stop just as we could be picking up momentum. We might think, "They don't know me so why would they want to help?" or "They probably get asked this all the time." But do we know for sure that they do not want to help or cannot help? Perhaps they would like to get to know you and they are afraid to ask or introduce themselves. How do you know they get asked all the time? You probably don't, because you are not them. Your greatest loss is that their answer could have been yes. You see, unless you ask, the answer is always going to be "no."

In communicating with others we can ask for assistance, answers, actions, or items. We can ask with intention and with reason. When you ask, you also allow others to ask for what they want. People want to be a part of something bigger, something more meaningful and contribute to their society. In general, people would rather be asked then told to do something.

What Does an ASK Do for You

Think about what your "ask" can do for you and also what it can do for someone else. When you ask for what you want, you:

- engage others
- create opportunities
- get direction
- increase your confidence
- create value

- build trust
- show appreciation
- eliminate confusion
- open discussion
- think critically
- being a new perspective
- challenge assumptions
- gather support

Asking for what you want has many benefits. Your "ask" matters! As Nancy Willard has said: "Sometimes questions are more important than answers."

Years ago, Walt Disney wanted to learn how he could improve Disneyland, so he engaged his employees by proposing a project and asking for their input. He received idea after idea. He took into account each of those ideas and created the Disney brand you see today. He continued to move forward with some of the ideas that others thought of. If he did not implement some of those ideas, he may have even gone bankrupt. The whole Disney organization philosophy is to involve their people and make them valued members of the team no matter where they are in the organization.

This concept is no different when it comes to engaging others in your dream or vision. They too would like to be a part of your success. If they knew they were able to help you in some way to get there, when you reach success they will know they were a part of the process.

You may wonder why and when you should ask for what you want. Here are some of the reasons:

- need assistance
- learn new things
- take action
- need something
- get clarification

Asking "why" is also very powerful. It allows you to think critically, at a deeper level, and helps you discover your true intent. Why don't more people ask for what they want? Some people think others should just know what they are thinking. You can't assume that people can read your mind. Remember they aren't you. That is why it is so important to be clear on what it is you want. Some people believe they don't have to ask and they think they are entitled to what they want while others refrain from asking because they are worried about another person's reaction. There are times you may avoid asking for what you want because you do not think you are worthy of receiving or you think you are being selfish by asking. Asking is a strength.

The greatest leaders engage their employees, communities, and organizations by asking good questions. These questions make others feel important and make them feel that they are making a difference. Are you asking enough questions?

How to ASK for What You Want

The ASK is not the hardest part of the question. When you ask for something that you want, you must do it knowing that you are worthy to receive it and you deserve what you are asking for. If it was to benefit your children, I would bet you would make an "ask." Why not for yourself? At the end of the day, when you ask for yourself, your children will also benefit as you reap the rewards. You need to ask politely and understand that the answer could be no. "No" does not necessarily mean "never." "No" is not something you should take personally. It just means not today. If every salesperson quit after hearing the word no, there would never be a true sales culture.

To increase your odds of getting what you want, do your research and learn the responses to anticipated questions. Take time to really know and understand the benefits of your product. When you speak with confidence, you remove doubt and resistance from the person you are asking.

"Ask for what you want and be prepared to get it."
—Maya Angelou

There are details you need to remember:

- People may be waiting for you to ask them because of their own fears and internal chatter. People naturally want to help people.

- Your ASK can also lead to more asks, new friendships, joint ventures, and introductions to people you *should* know.

- **Be very clear in asking for** what it is you want.

Know that your ask matters and makes a difference.

Know that your ask matters and makes a difference. An example from my own life is the shoebox campaign my husband and I spearhead each year. Several years ago, I was reviewing my bucket list. One of the items on the list was to be sponsored to deliver shoeboxes with my family to the orphanages in Ukraine and see the children open shoeboxes filled with gifts.

We have sent shoeboxes overseas to the orphanages in Ukraine for many years, but because my children were small at the time I realized that I would not be going to Ukraine anytime soon. I had wanted to make the trip to deliver the shoeboxes to the orphanage so we could see the children faces light up as they opened the boxes. One day, I had an "ah-ha" moment while reading my church bulletin. There was a need at a school right here in my own city. There are many needs in our own backyards where we can create our opportunities. I called the school in my area, shared my dream, and asked if I could support their school. Guess what? They said, "YES!" We were able to re-create Christmas morning with children dressed in pajamas as they all opened their gifts (shoeboxes) filled with toys, socks, toques, mitts, a snack, juice box, toothpaste, and toothbrush. There was one catch. The children could not open their boxes until every child was seated with a decorated shoebox in front of them. Santa, the elves, and I sang "We wish you a Merry Christmas and a Happy New Year!" and then we all shout out a 3-2-1 countdown where all the children open their boxes at the same time. The gym burst with energy and excitement as they all open their gifts. I also learned that the vice principal's mother was the coordinator for shipping the shoeboxes to Ukraine. See you never know how close you are to the contact you may need to make your dreams come true.

We originally started helping 120 children 5 years ago. Now a simple bucket list item has grown to serve close to 1300 children. In year 2, we were asked if we could feed the children a meal. I was not sure how we were going to go about it but all I envisioned was one of those children in front of me and how could I say no. I got off the phone with the vice principal and sent an email to all of our family and friends to ask for help. One of my family members suggested the local culinary school. We contacted them and they were happy to prepare all the food. All we needed to do next was ask for donations of turkeys, potatoes, and vegetables. It all came together – coincidence? I don't think so.

Later, we were able to provide even more meals. During one of my triathlons, I met Frank Santiago from Jitterbee pancakes. I approached him and asked him in a long winded energetic phone message if he would be interested in supporting our cause. He met with my husband and he has helped us ensure the children are fed for over 3 years.

It has really turned into quite a production from a pancake breakfast to Christmas carols by our elves (volunteers) and a visit from Santa and Mrs. Claus (aka me) to watching the children open their gifts. For some of these children, what we give is the only gift they receive during the season.

One year, a reporter who was covering the event, had grabbed her story and was ready to make off to the office when my husband pleaded with her to stay for an extra 20 minutes so that she could experience the Spirit of Christmas with us. She stayed and in the midst of all the excitement one of the elves handed her a gift to hand out. She knelt down by a little girl and wished her a Merry Christmas. As she handed her the gift, the little girl's eyes became as bright as shining stars then she asked "What is this?" The child beside her exclaimed, "Why it is a gift!" The inquisitive little girl said, "I have never received a gift before." Out of the corner of my eye, I saw the reporter burst into tears.

We shared a glance and tears fell down my face as well. For the joy of seeing the children faces light up can be overwhelming.

The ripple effect it has had on our family, colleagues, and friends has been tremendous. We share our story and invite others to be a part of it. Now we have people asking us about how they can be a part of it. It has been amazing. We have had organizations, school leadership teams, and individuals step up wanting to help. We do not market this event. Every year, we start with nothing and end with nothing other than incredible memories and handmade cards from children. If I had not asked for what I needed, the warmth I feel in my heart and the smiles and the tears I saw on the children faces and volunteers would not have come to pass.

How many people are waiting for you to ask? How many people want to be a part of your success story? How much better would the world be if you only made the ASK? Your ASK matters. Let others in on your ASK. Be prepared for them to give you a resounding, "YES!"

Five "Rights" of Asking for What You Want

1. Right Reason

Make sure you know the reason why you are asking for what you are. You don't want to be coming from a selfish place, where you would ask anything to get what you want and perhaps do anything to get what you want no matter what the price, even if it was at the expense of others. When you create situations which involve win-win opportunities, you can also give others what they may want. Everyone comes away satisfied. You must take action that is aligned with your values.

2. Right Question

You must be clear on what it is you are asking for. You want to be as specific as possible so that you can guarantee that when you get a yes, you get exactly what you wanted. Time is precious so you need to highlight important facts and ask specifically for what you want. The more clarity to your question, the more likely you will receive a yes. You also need to know the background about what you are asking for. You will appear to be more confident and you will likely get a better response.

3. Right Method

What is the best method of asking for what you want? You may choose to contact people by e-mail or phone, but face-to-face conversations are usually the best. Face-to-face conversations offer an opportunity for eye contact and body language. This is also the best way to ensure that you are asking with sincerity and respect. You need to be fully present when you ask, with no distractions. Believe you can get what you are asking for.

4. Right Timing

Your timing can be everything. It is important to see if you can set up a time to speak to whoever it is you want to ask, without distractions. Sometimes you may need to ask more than once because at the time you did ask, they have may have been tired at the end of their day, just returned from a meeting, or even a heated discussion. Ensure that when you're asking, the time is good for the person you are asking.

5. Right Person

Asking the right person will provide you with the greatest opportunity to hear the word *yes*. You want to ask the person who has the authority to give you what you want or direct you to where you need to go to find your answer. Just like a business meeting, you want the right people at the table at the right time for the right issue at hand. You need to ask a person who already has the knowledge you need or knows someone who can help you.

"You can't ask for what you want unless you know what it is you want. A lot of people do not know what they want or they want much less than they deserve. First you have to figure out what you want. Second, you have to decide that you deserve it. Third, you have to believe you can get it. And, forth, you have to have the guts to ask for it."

—Barbara de Angelis

There are many things you may want to ask for yet you may not know the: Why? Who? When? Where? What? Take time to think about what it is you want and ask yourself the following questions:

- What will asking do for me?
- Can I ask in a way that everyone benefits?
- What is stopping me from asking for what I really want?
- Why might I be afraid to ask?
- How will my asking also improve the lives of others?
- Do I know what I must ask for in order to achieve what I want?
- What actions must I take to get what I want?
- Do I know who to ask for assistance or direction?

15 Things Ask For

1. to interview an expert in a field of interest
2. an opportunity to collaborate
3. volunteer at a homeless shelter
4. assistance from a virtual assistant
5. someone to be your accountability partner
6. how you can assist someone else
7. an introduction or referral
8. donation for a charity
9. someone to watch the kids so you can go to a networking meeting
10. feedback on your marketing before you give your marketing a makeover
11. someone to be a guest blogger on your website
12. sending a press release to local media to create awareness about your business
13. sponsorship for clothes, printing, or merchandise
14. advertising opportunities

There are many things you can ask for. It is a matter of knowing what it is you want and knowing that whatever you ask for matters. You never know the impact of your ask.

Daniella asked a local spa owner if she could collaborate with them by asking them to serve her teas to their clients while they were waiting in between services. The spa clients loved her teas and started to contact her directly to purchase more. The spa became known for creating an experience that other spas did not offer. A win-win!

What do you have to offer that creates an experience like no other?

Chapter 3

From Mom to Celebrity—Getting Yourself Noticed, Known, and Remembered

"Those who are blessed with the most talent don't necessarily out-perform everyone else. It's the people with through follow-through who excel." —**Mary Kay Ash**

Soon after starting your business, you may have had moments when you asked yourself, "Oh my gosh, what have I gotten myself into?" You may have cried in the shower or woke up in the middle of the night thinking "What did I do to get where I am? What's the impact it's had on my family?" There are so many new things to learn and do that you may have lost track of them when you got caught up in the excitement of making the decision to be an entrepreneurial mom.

First of all, I just want to tell you that I have been that mom! I have had those moments where I questioned every action, wondering if there was going to be a payoff. I am here to tell you that when you are clear on what you want and if you persist and are consistent you can succeed. You can be there as your children are growing and need you, *and* you can grow a successful business.

This chapter is focused on how you can position yourself in today's digital marketplace and infuse both offline and online techniques. I will show you how to stand out in the marketplace, share your products, services, and message, create opportunities to serve others, and make money in the process. This is how a mom becomes a celebrity in her own backyard and beyond.

Systems and Processes

With any successful business, you need to create systems, processes, checklists, forms, and templates to streamline your business functions. Why reinvent the wheel every time? You may do things automatically without even giving it a thought. How much easier would it be to delegate some of the items on your plate to someone else?

Ensuring that you have effective processes in place will allow you to make time for your family *and* your business. If you create and explain the process and the way you like things done, it will be easier to hire a team and allow yourself to work on focused projects, putting your skills where they really need to be.

What you want to grow must be measured.

Do you have a daily action plan, marketing plan, or sales projection? How are you going to reach your goals?

Create an action plan like the one below. Keep in mind that consistency is the key.

ACTION	DESIRED OUTCOME	RESOURCES	DEADLINE
What action(s) do you need to take?	What is your desired outcome? Your "why" for taking action.	What resources are accessible to you? Who do you need to ask for help?	When do you want to accomplish it by?

Action plans are just one of the things you can do to keep yourself focused, manage your time, and get clear on future steps you need to take. What you want to grow must be measured. Keep track of what money is coming in and what money is going out, the traffic to your website, and the conversion from website visitor to paying customer. Because of my nursing background, I refer to this as VITALS: the pulse of what is happening in your business. You need to know the numbers in order to shout, "Show me the money!"

Jenna, a personal trainer, started using an action plan and realized how much more intentional and focused her actions became. She started a biweekly online newsletter and hired a virtual assistant to format it and take care of sending it out. Her customer database grew as people loved what she shared every two weeks with her newsletter. She even started to add promotions and events to it. The more her database grew, the more money that came into her business. Jenna offered value by giving the people in her database what they wanted. She was there to help them live a healthier lifestyle. With her action plan, Jenna was sowing seeds of her success.

Sow the Seeds for Success

Sowing seeds of success may sound like you're gardening or farming. You may not be Johnny Appleseed, but the analogy is so revealing to one's success. You may think, "How does sowing seeds actually apply to me?" In business, the more you build relationships, the more people who learn or know of your business (your list), the greater your revenue stream will be.

Sowing the seeds of success is not an overnight process. There is no pill or magic bullet solution here. Have you ever planted a seed in a garden or watched a crop being put in the ground? Neither the gardener nor the farmer comes out in the next morning preparing for harvest. The seed requires the nutrients from the soil, water, and the glorious sunshine in order to grow and stretch to the sky. You, too, need to grow your knowledge and nurture the relationships you build. During the process you also learn and grow into the person you were meant to be.

> *Seeding is letting others know about your business and learning how you can help them.*

What is seeding and how does a person seed? A seed is defined as a source or beginning. The same is true in your business; you are creating and nurturing new beginnings and relationships with others. Some relationships will develop and flourish and some with not grow at all and that's okay. Some relationships need to be reseeded as you may have had a misunderstanding or you may have lost touch with the other person. Seeding is about letting others know about your business and how you can help them. They want to know about the results you create. You, in turn, will grow your business.

Here are several ways to sow the seeds of success:

- Take a genuine interest in people and learn about them. What makes them tick? What is *their* "why" for doing what they do? Look for the common thread between you and them. People appreciate that you take time to care about them as a person not as a commodity.

- Follow-up with a phone call (preferred) or e-mail to connect with people following a meeting within 24 to 48 hours of meeting them.

- Send a card of appreciation to your current client base.

- Utilize direct mail marketing with postcards or brochures (not as common any more but it has greater impact due its novelty).

- Create articles or blogs that provide content with tips, strategies, and techniques that will benefit your followers.

- Speak at conferences, trade shows, or associations to get yourself out there. The more your name and brand are out there the more people will start to learn about you.

- Collaborate with others in cross-promotion of each other's businesses. Word of mouth marketing is continually one of the most powerful marketing methods.

Essentially, you are marketing by sharing your knowledge, products, and services.

Make a list of fifty ways you can get the word out about your business.

Here are a few just to get you started:

1. Social media (Facebook, Twitter, LinkedIn and YouTube)
2. Online newsletter
3. Print newsletter

4. Opt-in on your web page

5. Business cards (use the back too!)

6. Newspaper advertising

7. Radio

8. Television

9. Charity functions (donate a product or service)

10. Your email signature (have a call to action)

Continue to make your list; there are so many ways to get the word out!

How do your clients find out about the products and services they use?

You cannot sow just a few seeds, stop, and suddenly start to reap the rewards of growth. You must plant seeds regularly and consistently so you can grow connections and opportunities. Ensure you are intentionally sowing the seeds of success by connecting with people who are aligned with your values and you will start to see the seeds grow. Think about how your clients or customers find out about the products and services they use. Better yet poll or ask them! The seed you plant today could be the treasure you reap tomorrow.

Developing Your Persona On and Offline—Be the Expert

You can develop credibility as being a person who walks her talk and creates the results that people are looking for. You can solve the problem that is holding them back from achieving whatever it is they are after. You are a woman who takes action and has learned from experience.

What skills do you have that you may be dismissing because you see someone else as "knowing" so much more?

When establishing yourself as an expert, it is so important to align with your brand, and separate yourself from the masses of people who put their shingles and claim to be expert in their area. You want people to be attracted to you because you provide them with a solution or information to improve their lives or businesses in some shape or form.

Many people speak and motivate, however some of them fall short failing to provide practical useful information that people can walk away with and improve today. I listened to a presentation one time where the speaker was sharing information about her business, but never shared what she could do for her audience or what they could learn from her as an example. After the presentation, she made an offer to continue to do business with her but I did not feel that she gave me anything I could use or implement in my business. When you can give people tips and tools or products or services that they can use immediately to affect change in their lives or businesses, they will hire you or refer you.

You can develop your persona through your marketing. Do you want to grow your business and taste how sweet success can be? You will definitely want to learn about marketing pie! Marketing is an important part of your business operations. Your marketing strategy is the part of your business that attracts clients to you and your products and services. It is how they get to hear about you and get to know you. Marketing helps you build your list or database, and then allows you to key in your follow-up.

The marketing pie is a tool I use to help me focus on my business and plan for my day, month, and year. To help you understand the marketing pie, get a piece of paper and a pen. Draw a circle and draw a line through the middle horizontally and then vertically. Draw a few more lines dissecting the center of the circle just like you would be slicing a pie. Let's start with six slices. Each slice of the pie is a marketing tool that you use to attract more customers by serving them with valuable content to boost their business's bottom line.

Here are six ways you can build your list and share your expertise with your potential customer:

1. **Opt-In Box on your website**. Offer a free report, e-book, tele-class, video series, or podcast. If you do not have an opt-in

box, you must get one as soon as possible and offer the guests to your site something of value. A way they get to know you and what you do.

2. **Website, Blog and/or Ezine.** You can website and blog should showcase your expertise. This a great way for people to learn about your business. An electronic newsletter keeps your clients and prospects in the know about what you are up to. You can share articles, blog posts, testimonials, tips, or techniques. Ezines can be sent out every week, biweekly, or monthly. I find biweekly is the best way to stay top of mind.

3. **Video**. Create short, two-minute videos that offer three to five tips related to what you offer your clients. This is a very powerful tool!

4. **Social Media**. Twitter, Facebook, and LinkedIn are the top venues for sharing yours events, articles, blogs, and other valuable content with others. Not only can people like or comment on your postings, they can share your posts with their followers.

5. **Direct Mail**. You can utilize postcard marketing to get the word out about your business and provide a free offering to a special report, e-book, or download.

6. **Teleseminars**. Offer a thirty to sixty minute teleseminar teaching your clients and prospects about something that they can be doing in their business or their life. This is a great way for them to also get to hear your voice and get to know you.

Tradeshows, seminars, or workshops are others.

To start with, focus on two or three pieces of the marketing pie until you have successfully used them before moving on to others. You do not want to spread yourself too thin and dilute your message. Now what piece of the pie would you like?

Get Out of Hiding

It's easy to get caught up in social media marketing and the security of being behind your desk. But you need to step out of your comfort zones and meet people face-to-face. No matter how much technology grows, people still like connection and conversation. You are better able to understand someone's tone and body language in person. Leadership guru Robin Sharma suggests that we should get rid of desks altogether. You need to be where the people are. Pay attention to where the people you serve are spending their time. You should be there too.

We talked about the importance of communicating and how to network in chapter two. You need to ensure that you put these skills to use. Research networking breakfasts, luncheons, or dinners that may be available in your community. Not sure where to find them? Check into your local Chamber of Commerce or go to www.meetup.com to find a networking group in your area. Go to a variety of them and see which ones fit best for you to expand your network. Different groups have different people with different needs. Why limit yourself?

Let people sample your services with a complimentary offer or a discount for their first visit or purchase. How else will people get to know like and trust you as a business owner?

Consider volunteering in your community. As your business grows you may even consider sponsoring some events. You could sponsor your child's soccer or hockey team. People will be more likely to do business with you because they see you as a person who is not just interested in getting their money but is also interested in giving back to the community.

One of the greatest things you can do is to collaborate with another business through cross-promotion. There are tons of ways to cross promote your business. For example, a baby clothing store may want to collaborate with a photographer. The clothing store can have a special promotion from the photographer posted at their store. The photographer can promote the clothing store's upcoming sales or location. These create win-win situations that don't have to cost money, other than partnering up in promotion and helping get the word out.

You may also consider asking other businesses to sponsor you. I have had a number of small retail stores outfit and accessorize me for speaking events or appearances. In turn, I announce where my clothes or accessories come from to promote their businesses.

Does Your Website Need a Facelift?

There is nothing worse than going to someone's website and seeing that they have not done anything to it for years. If your website looks outdated or stale, it looks as though you're not in business. When people are given a choice, they choose a website that is current and up-to-date. You also need to ensure that your website can be found. Google is my greatest research assistant and the number one place where people learn more about products and services—and your competition. Make sure your website is listed! Make sure you are not a "best kept secret."

When considering giving your website a face lift, you want to consider the following questions:

- What experience do you want your customers and prospects to have when they visit your site?

- How can you share your story? Be someone they can identify with. Perfection can be intimidating.

- What benefits will people gain from working with you or using your product?

- Do you have an irresistible offer for your visitors?

- What do you want to your customers or prospects to know, do, or purchase when they come to your website?

As you gain a clearer perspective of what you want your end result to be, you will be able to create a website that is congruent with your brand as the best represents you. You will also save yourself time and money by targeting your website and the voice of your content to the audience you wish to serve. Surf the Internet and check out other websites in your industry. What do you like and what do you not like?

Incorporate the things that you like and that make you unique in the marketplace.

Videos

Make sure to use videos and pictures. Video is one of my favorite ways to connect with others virtually. Not only do they get to know your personality, but you can engage, entertain, and educate your audience. Video is a way that you can create an experience and tell a story.

People are attracted to interaction as visual information. They are looking to be educated and entertained as well as engaged. Video is one way in which you can build credibility and trust with your viewers. You should have a professional welcome video on your homepage explaining why people should be spending some time on your site and give them a call to action which can be adopted e-zine at the free special report, teleclass, or webinar. Remember to share the benefits and how you can help them.

The most important part of creating your video is remembering to just be yourself and allowing your personality to shine through. You may start on by asking 2 to 3 questions of challenges that your viewer may be experiencing right now, explain how you can relate to where they are right now (empathy is powerful), and share 3 to 5 tips, tools, and techniques for how to be the solution to the challenge. You will also want to offer a call to action. This call to action could be learning about new resources on your website, purchasing one of your products or services, or opting in for your e-zine or webinar. Suggest to your viewers that they need to share your video. Keep your videos short, sweet and to the point.

If you are finding it difficult to develop a video, you may wish to try a video slide creation website such as www.animoto.com. You can add music to your photos and create unique video slide shows to share with others for free.

Blogging, Newsletters, and Ezines

Does your website connect to your blog? A blog is a platform of communication that is used for discussion and sharing information with others. According to Wikipedia, there are 172 million identified blogs and 1 million new posts being produced each day.

Blogging is a great way to not only build your list but share valuable content as well. There are many different blogging niches such as corporate blogs, hobbyist blogs (food, crafts, and fashion as an example), and self-employed bloggers like you. According to Technorati's blogging statistics, 65% of blogs are taken more seriously than ever before. A blog is usually used with another form of social media. The digital entrepreneurial mom can use blogs in combination with platforms such as Facebook and Twitter to drive traffic to her website.

Some of the key pieces you should having your blog include:

- a catchy or snappy title (statement or question)
- ask questions so your reader can relate to your content -what are their challenges or questions they may be asking you
- 3 to 5 tips or tools that people can use right now
- ensure your blog is shareable
- a call to action -ask them to comment on or share your post

The ezine or electronic newsletter is an inexpensive way to reach and build your following. You must build your list. Your electronic newsletter is no different than the ones you receive through direct mail. You can design it the way you want and format it so you are offering valuable tips to your readers. You may even add in video. Many of the email marketing websites have templates that make it easy for you to insert your content. A few email marketing sites you may want to investigate are *Aweber, Mail Chimp, iContact, and Constant Contact.*

Electronic newsletters can be scheduled weekly, bi-weekly, or monthly. I have found that bi-weekly usually will suffice depending on your audience. You want to be on top of mind of your readers so they can think of and refer you to others or to rave about the valuable content you share.

Check out what others in the same industry are talking about on their **blogs or websites**. Pay attention to the comments posted by readers. The comments may generate a few solutions you could write about. Write a **book review or recommendation** about one of the books you just read and share the lessons you took away from it with your audience. Make sure you Tweet or Facebook the author –they usually appreciate feedback. Share some of your **challenges or celebrations** you have encountered while running your business. What are some of the **headlines of the magazines** you read? What are your **audience's needs or what questions do they need answers to**? Be the solution. Send out a survey and ask your readers what they want or need to know! Content is everywhere. What you think is simple, someone is still learning.

Decide how frequently you want to send out your e-zine—weekly, biweekly, or monthly. Select a theme or topic you want to touch on for the month and then break it down. This exercise will help you stay motivated and keep focused on creating content. Creating content can be fun and profitable especially when it grabs your readers' attention.

QR Codes or Snap Tags?

A QR code is a digital image that can be scanned by a smartphone and directs you to information or a web page to allow for opt-in and valuable information. A Snap Tag works the same way but instead of a digital image of square to scan, you can have people scan your logo or a design that looks more aesthetically pleasing to the eye. Consider including a QR Code or a Snap Tag on your business card and invite people to scan the code to be taken immediately to your website, where they could sign up for your newsletter or receive a free offer (special report, audio download, free CD, or podcast). Keep in mind that not everyone is familiar with these, so you need to be able to provide direction of what applications they may need to download in order to scan or read the codes. These wonderful tools are great ways to tie your business card in with your website.

You can create QR codes for free by just doing a search for QR code creator or generator. There are several options.

Twitter

This is a form of micro blogging in which post must be 140 or less. Think of your target market and how you can target your message to your audience. It is a great way to build conversation, make connections globally, and share valuable content with your followers. There are more and more ways to share thoughts and ideas and quotes when you are walking through the mall, dropping your kids off at school, or while you are getting a pedicure. We live in a mobile world and there are many ways in which you can share your message and increase your credit credibility as an expert.

There are even ways in which to customize your Twitter page. I have seen many people create twitter backgrounds that promote their brand as well as their message.

In the Huffington Post article "Twitter Statistics Show Stunning Growth" (2011), the author mentioned that Twitter had a 182 percent increase in the number of people tweeting and sharing information. This is a huge phenomenon in which you can be a part of. So as you can see, social media is a resource you need to tap into. Your marketing does not have to be costly to share your message.

Facebook

Facebook is a platform in which you can have a personal and professional page. Your professional page is your fan page where you ask followers to like your business. In order for people to like your business you need to provide valuable information in which intrigues your followers to sign up for your e-zine or follow your blog. Eventually some of these followers may become your customers. Post images, quotes, current thoughts, support causes, and share events such as teleseminars, webinars, and live events. Make sure that you keep the conversation going. You want to thank people for commenting on your post. Perhaps your post provoked a question you can answer. The conversation may also stimulate ideas for you to create a blog post.

One of the great things I love about Facebook, is you can promote your events, products, and even your fan page through Facebook ads. There are options for pay per click or an opportunity to target your promotion by location, occupation, and age group and interest and pay a flat fee. Again, look at what you are trying to achieve. The greater the list you build, the greater your network, the greater opportunity you have to build customer relationships that generate revenue.

Surf the Learning Curve and Grow Your Influence

By surfing the learning curve in the digital world, I mean surfing the net or using Google to help you learn what you need to learn to move ahead. Entrepreneurial moms can get hung up on the how, even though the resources may be a click away versus many phone calls or referrals. Be proactive and do some research into what you need. Your research will also help you gain clarity and ask better questions.

Trudy was looking for more ways to market her jewelry parties. She decided to research "how to have a successful jewelry party." She gathered tons of information and incorporated the training she had gained from the company and closed her best sales ever and booked four more jewelry parties for the next month. Trudy quickly moved up the ranks and became an executive director.

Bonnie owned a tire company. She researched all the car dealerships in her area and consistently marketed on social media and offline events. She started to collaborate with some of the car dealerships in the area. She researched information on her tires, articles, and blog posts about what people should know before purchasing tires. Bonnie has shifted her perspective from selling to educating her customers on their needs and what the benefits are. Doing her homework helped her put more money in the bank!

The learning curve of being a business owner can definitely seem overwhelming. As a business owner, you are responsible and accountable to yourself for learning the tricks, tools, and techniques of becoming a successful business owner. One of the best ways to hold yourself accountable is to tell a few people closest to you will you know you can trust and support you to help keep you on track and improving the learning curve.

Connect with other moms in business to bounce ideas off each other and to act as accountability buddies to each other. This way you can both learn and grow together. You may even break down tasks that need to be accomplished, such as research that would help your businesses grow.

As in other areas of time management, you also need to block off time for learning. This is what I like to refer to as "learn so you can earn." Give yourself a deadline to learn the information that you want to learn. Otherwise it is too easy to postpone the work, thinking you can learn it later. Obviously if it is something that has been brought to your attention to learn, you need to do something about it. Once you learn new information, to ensure that you're absorbing it the best thing you can do is try to teach it to another person, such as your accountability buddy.

Continuous learning and research will lead you to becoming known as an expert. By researching information on a topic of interest for your audience, you become known as the "how to" or the "resource" person. There are many people who have been successful at e-book publishing and at low cost. They research information, create a document, get it formatted, and post it on their websites or through ClickBank.com. (ClickBank is a digital marketplace that also offers an affiliate network.)They have learned to position themselves in the marketplace as credible experts on their topic of choice.

You can do this too. What does your customer want or need? What are some of the common questions you get asked? Gather ten of them and research the answers questions and then throw in your own spin on things. You then have 10 chapters of an e-book. You can then re-purpose the information and create an audio recording or workbook to go with it. Suddenly, you have an e-course. Each chapter could be a teleseminar, webinar, or teleclass. As you can see, the possibilities are endless.

As an entrepreneurial mom, I have used Click Bank to digitally promote my product. This method allowed my followers to have access to downloads in which they could lessen their learning curve quickly and efficiently. There are minimal start-up costs to working online and the best part is you can run your business anywhere in the world while having the flexibility to attend your family. Your business can be portable and you would be considered to be a laptop mom.

Subscribe to industry magazines, read books, or articles that can keep you abreast of what is going on in your industry and how you can be on the cutting-edge. Listen to audio books or speakers at conferences. Take notes while you listen and asterisk or highlight some of the things you need to learn or apply to your own business.

Get a Business Coach

One of the greatest investments I made in myself and my business, was to hire a coach to help grow my business. When I first started my business, I was not in a position to hire a coach. But as my business grew, I knew it was a necessity if I wanted to take my business to the next level. Here are handful of benefits a coach will give you:

- helping you gain clarity and focus
- holding you accountable for what you say you are going to do
- identifying ways in which you may be holding yourself back
- creating a plan with you to help meet your goals
- offering the next steps you may need to take in the process
- encouraging you and supporting your strengths
- sharing their wisdom, expertise, and how you can implement what they have learned or experienced into your own business

Remember that coaching is about taking actions. It's not counseling.

When the time is right for you and you have the finances available, hire a coach who is aligned with your values, has done what you want to do, and can share and give you the tools that will help you grow. This is why I love to coach others. There is so much satisfaction in helping people meet their goals

Chapter 4

Walking the Tight Rope of Business and Life Balance

"I believe that being successful means having a balance of success stories across the many areas of your life. You can't truly be considered successful if your home life is in shambles." —**Zig Ziglar**

Do you ever feel that demands of balancing your family, your business, and life are draining your energy? Even though you're working hard, do you still have trouble making ends meet and spending precious family time together? Do you ever compare yourself to someone who doesn't have a family and wonder if you will ever be successful?

The demands of having a family and running a business can be exhausting, but if you take time to create a sense of balance and harmony in our households and business, your business will soar. Balance helps us achieve the goals that we set for ourselves. It allows us to be creative and innovative and unleash new idea. It allows us on to focus on what we do best: implementation and delivery. Not only that, the family unit in embraces each other and is filled with joy and happiness. You can be successful growing a business, raising a family, and create a life that you love.

Mommy Guilt

As entrepreneurial moms, one of the most impacting emotions we feel is that of "mommy guilt." But guilt is a very unproductive emotion. There's no real return on investment and it simply wastes a lot of time and energy. Time and energy that you could be putting into spending time with your family your friends, and your business.

To get to the bottom of this emotion, you need to understand why you are feeling guilty. What needs are not being met? Are you feeling guilty because a stay-at-home mom who doesn't have a business made a comment about people who work and how they look after their families? Does it come from something your mother may have said? Or are you needing to tap into personal finances to grow your business and now it is impacting your family? Regardless, another person's opinion really is none of your business. You need to do what is right for you and your family.

Open communication with your family is important while running your business. Joanna, a mother of three, decided to start her own business so that she would have the flexibility to be home with her toddlers. Her mother-in-law commented that her housework was not being tended to in the fashion her son was accustomed to, and that having a business would interfere with raising her family. Joanna almost threw in the towel because she wanted to please her husband and his mother. She felt guilty because she thought that maybe her mother-in-law's statement was correct. Joanna did not want to negatively impact her family by starting a business.

Joanna decided to speak with her husband about his mother's comment to see if he felt the same way. Joanna's husband, Dave, said he knew it was important to Joanna to feel like she was contributing financially to the family, and to have an activity for herself. Dave stated that he would start becoming more involved in doing laundry and vacuuming. Joanna and Dave decided that they could sacrifice other luxuries and hire a cleaning lady to come for three hours once a month to help out. This action alone allowed Joanna to spend some concentrated time with her family as well as her business.

Three months later, Joanna's mother-in-law noticed a considerable change in her demeanor. She commented on how clean their house was and how unfortunate it was that she was unable to continue with her business because she knew that she had what it took to be very successful. Joanna smiled and explained that she and Dave had taken time to talk about their priorities and their values. They took time to define what was important to them and they decided to share the workload and ask for help when they needed it. Joanna's mother-in-law apologized and said that she should've been more supportive and was glad to see how happy she was and how happy her family was.

Not every circumstance is like Joanna's. No matter what circumstance comes your way; you have a choice to react both negatively or positively. Do not let mommy guilt extinguish the flame and the desire to serve that is burning inside of you.

It's important to not identify yourself as a mother alone. You also should not be identifying yourself solely by the work you do. Your work is a function, who you are is not. If your child acted up, do you feel bad about yourself or do you take the time to teach and nurture their behaviors? Do you react because you believe that others are judging you based on your children's behavior?

It is important for you to be you just for the sake of being you. Really what does mommy guilt do for you? Change your thinking and shift your thoughts to ones that are more productive and channel that energy and your love to your business and your family. Remember that creating balance is important and that stressful times are only temporary.

What Is Balance Anyway?

Before you can strive for balance, you first need to understand what balance means to you. Does a balanced life mean that you're tending to everything on your to do list? Does it mean that there is peace in your house and there is no evidence of sibling rivalry? Does it mean you're having romantic dinner by candlelight with your husband and toddlers in tow? Does it mean you have a business meeting with another business mom at the playground? Does it mean that you can go to a networking luncheon because you know someone is looking after your website or social media marketing?

What would it take for your business, your family, and your life to be balanced and you to feel joy and happiness?

When creating balance you need to decide what is truly important to you? The balance we are trying to create is the balance between many roles such as:

- being an involved parent
- being successful in our business
- creating healthy couple relationships
- caring for an aging parent
- being a leader in the community
- spending quality time with family and friends

- keeping a clean house
- giving back to causes that matter
- and of course, some me time

Balance is something I've been trying to achieve for many years. Several years ago, I felt as though I was running a marathon of looking after three kids under the age of five, working, and trying to look after myself. For weeks, my husband had been leaving early in the morning to take a class, and then going straight to work till midnight every day. One day, I was shuttling my children to their schools and dropping off treats for a Valentine's Day party. I was signaling to turn off the highway onto the street that leads toward my child's school when a car did not let me merge. Suddenly my world stopped. I hit a traffic sign in the median of the road. Our one-year-old minivan was in bad shape, and I all could do was sit there in tears.

The children were okay, and all I could think of was what my husband going to say. I contacted him and he came immediately from his class. I called my brother who lived nearby and he took the kids to their Valentine's Day party. I called my father and the only thing he said to me was, "Debra, do you think you have enough on your plate?" I had been trying to keep everything running smoothly even though it wasn't. The question was: at what cost?

Since that time, whenever I need to make a decision, I take a look at what is important to me and my family and ask myself, do I really need to add more to my plate? And if so, is there room? I look for harmony. Now I have created a much more organized and balanced life. Once you know what is important to you—you can make a plan!

1. **Determine what is important to you.** By knowing this you will be more conscious and aware of what is important to you and it will be easier to make decisions based on your values and your priorities.

2. **For one week, keep track of where your time goes.** Keep a time log. How long does it take you to complete a task? What tasks are you working on? Are you making the greatest use of your time? Identify where you can delegate, eliminate, or

complete items. Get things off your plate you have been putting off. If they're still there, ask, "What is expendable, and what is not? How important is each?"

Activity/ Task	Time Started	Time Finished	Duration	Return on Investment (Was this a revenue generating activity, time waster, or was there a potential to delegate this task?)

3. **Plan ahead.** Childcare, carpooling, date nights, meals, and even clothes for the next day. The more you plan, the smoother things go.

4. **Build what is important to you into your lifestyle.** If volunteering is important to you, find a way to volunteer and see if you can involve your family. Not only will this help develop family bonds, but it also creates treasured memories.

5. **Save money and time by realizing how precious life is and focus on what is important to you.** Block off time for yourself. Remember you cannot help other people when you cannot help yourself.

Plan Your Morning Routine

"If people were meant to pop out of bed, we'd all sleep in toasters."
—Garfield, the Cat

For many households, mornings are one of the most stressful times of the day, especially when you're trying to get the children out the door for school, and you are ready to start your day.

Children thrive on structure so it is important to create a consistent morning routine. Try to get up in the morning before the kids so you can exercise or grab that morning cup of coffee to allow yourself time for you to pray or meditate or just be alone with your thoughts or even just with your partner. Shower and get dressed before the kids get up. Get your children and yourself to set your clothes out the night before. This makes it less stressful to make a decision about what you're going to wear in the morning. Get backpacks and lunch prepared the night before too. This will leave a lot of stress in the mornings.

Here is a checklist.

Night before and as required:

- School
- Sign Agenda
- Sign field trip forms
- Fill out hot lunch forms
- Backpacks packed
- Lunches made
- Set out clothes for the next day
- Pull out any meat that needs to be defrosted for tomorrow's supper

Morning:

- Go for a 30 min walk
- Take a shower
- Make the kids breakfast
- Get kids off to school.
- Go to breakfast meeting.
- Marketing and research.
- Customer follow up
- Write new article
- Brief virtual assistant on upcoming project
- Client work

You can build all this into your Google calendar or iCal to block off periods of dedicated time to these areas. This is just one example of how to get things done.

Before you start your day, take a look at your to do list and look at what your priorities are for the day. Begin with those first. Brian Tracy refers to this as "eat that frog," where you get rid of the most difficult or avoided task first. Once you do this, your day is set and you have accomplished a huge task. Shift your language and thinking from the "have to" do to "I get to do." Notice the difference in your language. You have opportunities to create your outcome. Once you accomplish those, the rest of the day will feel like a breeze. Take time to plan your day.

Map It Out

One of the greatest business lessons I have learned is the need to create a calendar of the year to ensure that I plan out my vacations, free days, and working hours. Map out dates with your spouse and children, together and individually. When you map out the calendar of your life and business you'll avoid missing your kid's soccer games or ballet recital, you won't get surprised with a bake sale request the morning of the sale, and you won't miss an important meeting that supports your business.

My friends and family get a chuckle out of my color-coordinated, calendared fridge: my Grand Central Station. But it works for me. You need to find what works for you. For the digital mom's, you can sync your family members' calendars on their smart phones and computers through iCal or Google Calendar, then everyone knows what is going on. I use my Grand Central station and iCal. By doing this, I can be out at a meeting or a function where I do not have my paper calendar and I can grab my phone and make appointments. You can also save yourself a ton of time by planning your life this way and squeezing the most out of the time you have available. You can get super focused on how you take on your days.

Eliminate Time Wasters

There are many time wasters that steal away your attention and sabotage your productivity. Take a look at your to- do list and determine what items may be "other people's agenda." These items can be very time consuming and even drain some of your energy because you are not working on what you really want to complete for yourself and your business. Take charge of your time and energy in a whole new way by setting some boundaries by valuing your time.

Schedule specific times in which you plan to check your e-mail. For example, you could check it at 9:30, 11:30, 1:30, and 3:30 pm. I have a colleague who also lets people know she only checks her email at certain times of the day and if she needs to be contacted they should call. Not only is she productive but she set boundaries around her time.

If you are inundated with too many e-mail subscriptions, try to maintain only the ones that are most pertinent for you. Scan for the emails from people you are awaiting an answer from. These are emails related to your business. Unsubscribe to some of the newsletters that you receive that you never get a chance to read, or put them in folder marked READ LATER. Another option is to set up another email address to receive newsletters or vendor offers. Remove yourself from Facebook groups that are not your ideal audience, you do not resonate with, or turn off the notifications so your email box does not get flooded.

Set aside time to delete messages or have your assistant clean up the email flow so you can concentrate on what is most important.

There are many different apps out there that can restrict your time or even block you from surfing the Internet during times you are trying to focus on getting work done. 30/30 is a free productivity tool available on iTunes that helps keep you on track. You can set up your tasks and time them. An alarm will go off when your time is up so you can then move on to your next activity. Just imagine how much you can get done!

The Social Media Trap

Social Media is one area where you can really waste some valuable time. Don't get me wrong. There is much power in social media, but it is so easy to get caught up, watching to see if other people are paying attention to your posts, and whether they are liking, or, commenting on your posts. Social media is a powerful tool that you need to use in a focused manner in which the information that you are trying to share is targeted, valuable, and timely.

Be mindful of your time and the impact you want to create. Create a social media marketing plan for your business. Print off blank calendar templates and plan out two to three posts per day or every second day for the next thirty days. Preschedule these posts by using websites such as www.hootsuite.com or www.socialoomph.com. There are several different ways that you can pre-set some of your social media to be sent to Facebook, Twitter, and your fan page. You can then go onto the sites to monitor what is being commented on so you can reply and engage with your followers.

You can also plan out your blog schedule, writing time, and networking time using the calendar technique.

> ## *Shift your language and thinking from the "have to do" to "I get to do."*

Peace and Harmony within Your Family

You may have heard the saying that you begin your life with family and you end your life with family. It's so important to create an environment and relationships that create memories and are filled with peace and harmony.

Moms are the queens of multitasking; however it definitely helps when there's a supportive family environment where you can flourish. Your family may be your immediate and extended family members, friends, neighbors, coworkers, and employees. We live in a world where there is so much more mobility across the country and sometimes there is no family available. This is when we need to enlist friends, neighbors, and coworkers to help out with carpooling or even some babysitting challenges.

The time with your children is precious and goes by so quickly. One moment you are holding your precious baby in your arms, watching your preschool finger paint, and the next thing you know, you are listening to your teenagers blasting tunes, and then watching your child walk across the graduation stage. Take a look at your family calendar and remember you do not need to be on every committee at school or on a board in your community. You may need to choose to take on smaller roles so that you can ensure that you're spending time with the people that matter the most to you.

You also want to avoid overscheduling, which can increase your stress and affect how you communicate with your family, customers, and peers. Your kids may even get burnt out or get low grades because they are trying to concentrate on too many things. Your family may also end up eating more fast food which can be unhealthy. When you are stressed, your decision-making can be affected and you may not be the most warm welcoming and friendly person to be around. You are better able to respond to situations when you are calm and collected. To avoid overscheduling, you must also set boundaries with others. You can appreciate being nominated for a parent advisory committee; however, you still have the ability to say no.

Allow your child to participate in 1 to 2 activities and evaluate the time commitment. You want to be their cheerleader. Don't forget you still need time to help with homework and school projects. Give yourself the opportunity to be involved in your own extracurricular activity as well. You need an outlet in which you can recharge your energy so that you can create and innovate in your business and give back to your family.

Take an exercise class or sign up for that painting or cooking class you have been thinking about. When you have an outlet where you can have time for yourself, you can be more creative, innovative, and more productive. Maybe you can even take a class with one of your children.

I spend a great deal of time with my children after school shuttling them to and from activities since my husband work evenings and weekends the majority of time. I thought we were having quality time; however, each child voiced the need to spend more special time with me. To achieve this, my business coach, Pat Mussieux, suggested that I get a dry erasable calendar and map out my business activities, my children's activities, and then plan for special time with each child and my spouse. She also told me to have everyone in the family record their wins for the day. I had already been recording my wins daily but getting my family involved was remarkable. I bought a four month planning calendar and set everything up. I let each member of my family put a special sticker on the date they chose to mark it.

Each member in my family looked forward to their special time with me. I went mini-golfing with my boys, and shopping with my daughter. During one of my mini-golf games, Nathan and I scored a hole in one on the same hole. We were jumping for joy! Later that evening when I asked everyone to write down their wins, he said that making the calendar was his win. Tears welled up in my eyes. I had lost track of how important that individual time was in getting to know them as individual people. It was making them feel that they mattered just as much as everything else I am involved in, in my life.

Do you know your spouse's and children's favorite colors, food, movies, sport, hobbies, and outings are? Do you know what they like best about you? Do you know what their greatest accomplishments are? Do you know what their fears are? Take time to get to know each one individually. You probably know some of their strengths even weaknesses. What can you do to bring out their very best? The time you spend with your spouse or child could be an hour of television or an afternoon out. Figure out what works for you. Turn off the cell phone, computer, or telephone ringer if you need to. Be fully present in the moment. Block off time in your calendar for networking, writing, planning, vacations, and free days. Make a date!

Remember, do not deviate from this date even if you have an opportunity for a revenue generating activity; your family needs to know that they are just as important as other activities. No amount of money can replace the relationship you build and nurture within your family. When your family unit is cohesive and functioning well, so will your business.

Creating Healthy Couple Relationships

Although many of women would like the support of their spouse and partner, not everyone understands what our role is as an entrepreneurial mom, especially if your business does not sell a tangible product but a service.

Even though you have to be more cognizant about your wants and needs as you build your business, you can develop support by sharing your vision and speaking with words that assert success and persistence. If you do not believe you are going to make it, how can you expect someone else to?

Do not leave your spouse or partner in the shadows while you spend long hours developing your business or putting energy into the kids. You need to reconnect as a couple regularly to maintain and grow your relationship. Make time for each other. There are so many small but significant ways you can do this:

- talk to or e-mail each other throughout the day
- go for lunch and or arrange a dinner date
- go for a Saturday morning walk
- go to bed at the same time . . . you never know what could happen
- Leave love notes in lunches or places where he could find them throughout his day,
- turn off the cell phone, and give him your undivided attention
- share household chores, or better yet hire someone to do them so you can spend more time with your spouse or as a family.

Learn what your spouse's expectations and dreams are and how you can support them. Make sure you share what your expectations and dreams are and how you can work together supporting your family and reaching your dreams. When you are working as a unit or team with clear expectations, it will be amazing what you can accomplish.

Michelle asked her husband, Mark, what his expectations were for her as a wife, mother and business owner. Michelle then did the same of Mark as a husband, father, and employee. Michelle wanted time to create and innovate in her business but also wanted her husband to be more involved in helping around the house and being more involved in their kids' activities. Mark stated he wanted more time together as a couple, to get involved in an extracurricular activity, and coach one of their children's sports teams. Michelle had no idea that he wanted to do these things. This exercise allowed them to formulate a plan and come up with ways to support each other. By doing this, they both agreed that they were better able to support and envision their goals for their family coming to life.

Let your spouse or partner know that you appreciate their support and thank them for pitching in with the kids. When everyone is on board with the family mission, it can definitely decrease the stress and refocus on what is truly important.

Where's The Time Control Button

Time goes so fast when you're doing what you love! And as a mom in business your already multitasking and always one step ahead thinking about what you need to do next, but you must be careful that you don't lose precious time and leave your family along the way as you grow your business. In order to be successful you need to manage your time wisely and ensure that all areas of your life receive the undivided attention you wish to give them.

You need to set priorities and this can be done by having a family meeting so that you understand what your goals are not only for your business but for your family as well. When you operate from a place of understanding you can set common goals. There are five essential principles that you need to follow when trying to create the life that you love.

1. **Family/business goal alignment**. As a family unit and as a business owner coming from a place of understanding of expectations, and individual dreams, and goal setting, you can better align your business and life decisions and allow others to do the same. At the end of the day, the most common denominator in striving for a better life and future for your fami-

ly that involves freedom and flexibility to do what you want in order to meet everyone's needs including your own. Michelle and Mark were a great example of alignment. Learn what your children's goals are to and what support they would like.

2. **Prepare.** You want to structure your business and make your plans around your family and not the other way around. If you always put what's important to you – your *why* in focus, you will not come from a place of resentment and disappointment.

3. **Share.** Let your spouse and children in on your business development. When they have a clear picture of what it is you actually do and what your goals are, they will be more understanding of some of the deadlines that you need to meet and the outcome you wish to achieve. Once again this communication needs to focus on the family/business goal.

   Trina, a mother of a nine and an eleven-year-old, kept her family communication line open and let them know when she needed uninterrupted time in the evenings. Her family worked and played in other parts of the house until she was free. If they needed her they could text her cell phone or put a note under the door. One hour of focused time became very productive. Trina could then spend time playing games with the kids before bed knowing she took care of things that were on her mind. Trina admitted that she was more present in spending time with her kids as the distracting thoughts were taken care of.

4. **Care.** There may be times when you can get your family involved in your business. Depending on their age they can, they can stuff envelopes, create PowerPoint slides, file, or help out with the housework or laundry. Not only are you role modeling or providing skills for their future, butut you are also building confidence and helping develop a leader of tomorrow. When you involve your family, not only do they feel that they've contributed, but they also feel a part of your success.

5. **Celebrate.** We often missed out on some of our successes because we are busy multitasking and chasing the next achieve-

ment. Stop being so busy. Slow down go on a date night with your spouse or celebrate as a family because these are the people who have been waiting in the wings, being your cheerleaders, waiting for this day to arrive just as much as you have. They love you and they want to be a part of your success. Arriving at success is not much fun when you don't have the people you love the most to celebrate with. Take the time to make them feel just as important as the business you are growing and I assure you that you will start creating a life you absolutely love.

Establish a Routine Schedule

People who are not entrepreneurs often do not understand that when you are self-employed or working from home that you are indeed working. You may get phone calls or unexpected visitors thinking that you can run errands for them or take them to appointments on a moment's notice. Sometimes you can but there will also be times you cannot. If they call and make requests, let them either know that you are busy or suggest a different time. Your time is valuable. You will need to set business hours in order to set boundaries so that others can be more understanding of your time.

Not only are you setting boundaries, you are also creating a structure and routine for yourself to maintain organization and motivation. When you are more aware of your work time, you will be more productive. Make use of the technology at your disposal! I use the timer on my iPhone to block time to write, plan, or de-clutter. The timer helps me get focused. I often set it for 20-30 minute increments and then reassess. My productivity soars when I do this. I can also let my family know that I have a timer on, and I need to focus on getting a task done. Keeping them in the loop eases any mommy guilt waiting in the wings.

Imagine what you could do in twenty minutes:
- Write a blog entry or an article.
- Read up on a subject area you are trying to learn more about.

- Follow up with 1-2 potential clients.
- Write out thank you cards.
- Plan your day for tomorrow or the next day.
- Map out a calendar of tweets, blog posts, or Facebook posts.
- Go for a walk or doing some super sets of weights at lunch time.
- Plan your meals for the day.
- Take time to listen to music or read a good book.
- Sit in a relaxing bath.
- Call a friend.
- Read a bedtime story.
- Play a game of soccer or have your child to take shots on you in goal.
- Listen to the events of their day.
- Watch their favorite show with them.
- Spend time doing what your spouse or partner likes to do.
- Play a board game.

Twenty minutes here and twenty minutes there add up quickly and compounded over time can yield amazing results. Empowered engaged teams, better health, and stronger relationships are a few of the outcomes. The results you get in your business are a direct result of your productivity and your focus.

Three Ways to Increase Your Productivity

1. **Monitor Your Time on Telephone Calls**: Keep an eye on the time you spend talking on the phone, you can easily get off on a side track conversation. Save non-profit generating phone calls for after business hours or allot them into your calendar in advance. When you are working and focused on a certain project, let your phone go to voicemail and check it when you take a break.

2. **Decide if a Face-to-Face Meeting is Necessary:** Decide whether or not you need to meet someone in person for a meeting or is the meeting one you can discuss over the phone. A fifteen to twenty minute phone call can save a lot of time in travel and meeting time.

3. **Be a Continual Learner**: Do you have trouble finding time to learn and grow to further develop your business strategies? Listen to audio program in your vehicle so that you can learn and develop new ideas to implement into your business. A stale mind will produce the same results. Innovation and creativity are required for sustainability and growth in your business.

Start your day by eliminating the "mommy guilt" and the time wasters and distractions. Time management is about self-management and creating a harmony with the ebb and flow of life and business. Family goal alignment can act as a rocket booster to your business as the support is beneficial and lessens the guilt. When you get laser focused on what you wish to accomplish, you will create a momentum that helps you move in great strides. These strides will seem more like leaps as you challenge yourself and up your game. You will become more efficient and more productive in getting things done so you can take inspired ACTION!

Chapter 5

Penny Pinching to Dollar Rolling—Sacrifices to Successes

"Great achievement is usually born of great sacrifice, and is never a result of selfishness." —**Napoleon Hill**

In this chapter, I want to help you focus on the qualities of successful entrepreneurial mom; the sacrifices made today that create the successes of tomorrow: and the strategies you can use to position yourself in the market place.

Success leaves clues! These clues can be built into how you run your business, family and life. Each quality helps build your business.

Qualities of a Successful Entrepreneurial Mom

Successful entrepreneurial moms know that their decision to become an entrepreneurial mom is based on short-term sacrifices for greater long-term gains—success! Think of the lesson you teach your children when you're at the cash register of the grocery store, near all the candy. When your child pleads with you to purchase something, you know that instant gratification will not serve long-term gains in making healthy choices. The occasional treat is fine but if every time you went to the grocery store this became a pattern this would be a long-term problem not only for their dental health but also on your pocket book. Your child will definitely gain skills as they try a new approach each time and become a great negotiator in the process. It's the same for you.

Consistency. Successful moms in business have learned that they must continue to market their messages even through the toughest economic times. Think of the story about the tortoise and the hare. The tortoise won the race because he kept going—slow and steady but the effort was consistent.

One of my favorite examples of lack of consistency is that of a restaurant that had been recognized for great customer service and excellent food. Its business had flourished in the first three months it was open. However with their success, they became complacent. They stopped paying attention to the details that created their success: greeting their customers promptly, tending to their tables, and presenting their dishes beautifully. The restaurant closed down within eighteen months.

Be consistent in how you deliver your products and your services, customer service, and your message. You are your brand.

Patience. Patience is a virtue, but in today's world so many people want the instant gratification or the magic pill of overnight success. You need to be strategic in how you operate your business. Every seed you plan and every interaction you make should be with intention. You want to be a business that is not only successful but sustainable.

Discipline. Working from home does offer a lot of flexibility, but for many it can affect their motivation and how they structure their day. Just like a successful athlete, the entrepreneurial mom must have discipline in her life to create a structure that will help her succeed. Your efforts will compound over time and lead to the sweet success you desire. Tracking time and money help you get further ahead and help you resist wasting time or impulse shopping. You need to know what money is going out and what money is going into your business if you want to grow. You want to ensure that your resources are being used appropriately and that waste is eliminated. I have heard people rave over the latest "overnight success." But those people did not witness the many early mornings, late nights, and sacrifices over several months and even years that brought the "overnight success" to where they are today.

Determination. Focus on the end goal and on knowing with clarity what it is that you want. When you are determined and focused on your purpose you will reach that goal. You are determined that you will focus until you succeed.

Courage. It takes a lot of guts to try new things and think outside the box. Over time you will develop confidence as well as the courage to try even more things. People often see new ideas or actions as risky, but is it so risky when you develop a knowledge base in that area and you minimize those risks? This is called due diligence. Do your homework or research when developing your plans. Get feedback or ask people who have done what you want to do, and get the guidance you need to feel that you are making a good decision.

Wisdom. Wisdom is not just about being book smart or having a degree. It is about putting your life experiences and your intuition to work to make decisions that give you the greatest return on investments with your time and energy and money.

You can learn new things and increase your knowledge to become wiser. How wise you are is tested by the decisions and choices you make.

> ## *The decisions and choices you make determine how wise you are.*

Small Sacrifices for Long-Term Success

There are several start-up costs when starting a business and, unless you had money put aside for starting your business or took a business loan to get started, it is natural that you will have some debt. As you know, there is good debt and there is bad debt. Good debt leads to revenue generating activity. Bad debt is related to impulse shopping and making emotional decisions without thinking about the impact on your family and your business. When it comes down to the basics, you need to identify your wants and needs. Sometimes, you need to say "no" to some of your wants until a later date.

I know several people who have maintained a part-time job or worked full-time while building their businesses. Some people refer to this as "straddling and struggling" but I'd rather do that than go bankrupt. I have built my business this way. You want to ensure you are setting yourself up for success and only you know when the right time to let go of the "job" and focus fully on your business.

There will be sacrifices and there may even be times when you feel like giving up. How do you view yourself and business? What do you believe is possible for you? Sacrifices can build character in a person who knows what she wants. Some of the short-term sacrifices that moms have made to build their businesses are foregoing vacations, designer clothes, and nights out on the town. Women understand that as their business grows, more opportunities will be afforded to them. If they position themselves correctly, they can make more money than they did as an employee and still have the freedom and flexibility to spend time with their families and plan that vacation of their dreams. There may be some penny pinching along the way but remember "this too shall pass." You will position yourself for long term success.

A positive attitude and a deep desire to succeed will trump any lack of effort because some of the efforts or skills that you do not have, you can outsource. Initially, you may do some of these things yourself to save money and understand the process so that you can grow your business and allocate your money where you get the greatest return on your investment.

Priorities, Progress, and Accomplishments

In order to grow your business, spend time focusing on revenue generating activities. As a mom, I know how easy it can be to get overwhelmed with all the things we have to do from making beds, doing laundry, shuttling the kids to and from activities, and trying to get to a networking event. Focus on one thing at a time; the most important thing. My theory is simple "Always remember to breathe," and you can get through almost anything. Yes I know we are the queens of multitasking and you can get many things done but if you throw a load of laundry in and need to send an e-mail. Throw the laundry in and don't find something else to distract you and ensure that you go straight back to work. Better yet, save the laundry for a different day so that you can have your concentrated time on building your business. In actuality, you are compartmentalizing your time. Really, how is this any different than the structure provided in the school system. By establishing routines, you will be able to focus on what really matters at the moment.

Goals

Track your goals so that you stay on track. Adjust your course as needed. Know when you have reached a particular goal so you can celebrate. Here is an example of what you can do to set up your goals. You can then break down each of your goals into manageable and reasonable tasks and timelines.

MY GOALS

What am I wanting to achieve?	How will I measure this?	Can I Achieve This?	Is This Goal Realistic for Me?	When will I need to achieve this by?

> ## *Track your small victories as well as big ones.*

We have small successes every day, yet we often are too busy pursuing our next adventure without appreciating how far we've come. Track your small victories as well as big ones, so you can see your growth and maintain the momentum needed to reach your goals. You can even do this on a 3 x 5 index card: list the date, up to five accomplishments, and how they bade you feel. Capture the emotional connection to your goals and progress. When you have an emotional connection to what you wish to accomplish, you are more likely to achieve it. Remember to take note of any new opportunities that come your way.

Finances

It is so important for women to be abreast of the finances not only in their household but in their businesses. If this is an area of weakness for you, you should hire a bookkeeper to help you. Keep track of your finances daily. I have seen many women leave the finances to their husbands only to be overwhelmed by learning about finances if they divorce or lose their spouse. Your money is your business! Not knowing the finances, can really shake your world.

You do not necessarily need a fancy program to help you do this it can be as simple as an Excel spreadsheet or Numbers on a Mac. No matter what tools you use, you need to do this.

Start by making a list of your revenue streams: products, services, programs, and so forth then make a list of all the expenses you encounter (web hosting, design, Internet fees, memberships, networking lunches, car maintenance, and gas). Remember also to keep track of your mileage to and from any events or client meetings. You can then put these into a spreadsheet and keep track of them on a monthly basis. (You will also be more prepared for tax time!)

What you do not measure cannot grow because you will not know if your business is actually making money or not. You will not know whether or not you can invest more into your business. Don't forget to pay yourself first even if it is $10 or $20 dollars that you put aside. It will compound and grow with consistent effort.

In Darren Hardy's book, *The Compound Effect*, Darren shares a story of a magic penny. "If you had a choice between taking $3 million dollars cash this very instant and a single penny that doubled in value every day for 31 days, which would you chose?" If you have heard this incredible story, you would know that the single penny would be the winner hands down. When you do the math, you will learn that at day 29, you will reach the matching $3 million dollars and day 31, you will have $10,737,418.24. Happy dance time!

Why is it so hard for people to believe that there is power in a penny? Hardy will say because it takes so much longer to see the payoff. I think this is where instant gratification loses it worth.

Build the Team

Business owners who build sustainable businesses know that their success cannot occur in isolation. You may have heard the phrase that "It takes teamwork to make the dream work."

You need to quit trying to do everything yourself. When you're just starting out or do not have a great deal of revenue coming in, you try to do many things yourself to save yourself some money. But what I learned is your flame and your passion for what you're doing can easily get burnt out when you try to spread yourself too thin. You have so many people around you who want and need your attention: your child tugging at your pant leg, your spouse wanting some of your affection, and your customers wanting your products and services. In order to be able to give to others, you need to look after yourself and you need to build a great team.

The team you build needs to have members who believe in your dream and have your best interests at heart. Sometimes we just need to let go of control in order to watch our business grow and trust in the people we hired to do the job well without micromanaging them. They may have incredible ideas to share as they align with your vision. They may be a contract employee or they may be someone you retain for a long time. You want to hire people who are the "A" players and always give their best.

Some of the people you may need on your team are a web designer, an editor, a virtual assistant, an office manager, an accountant, bookkeeper, and even a lawyer. Each has a specific duty to help you in your business. For example, if you need a PowerPoint completed for a presentation, you could outsource to a virtual assistant through any number of sources, including: www.odesk.com, www.elance.com, www.guru.com, www.taskjeannie.com, or www.fiverr.com for support in that area. For online business management, you may contact www.virtuallyall.net. The point is, you do not have to do it alone.

You may have not even realized that you have a team who helps looked after the health of your family and yourself. You have the optometrist, a dentist, and a doctor and maybe even a personal trainer. They are all people helping you reach the end goal. Why not have a team of people help you grow your business and look after what matters to you just like your health.

Plan for Growth

You always need to be thinking about growing your business. This is why it's so important to be very clear on setting goals and targets.

You need to map out your plan and identify some of those obstacles that might come up along the way. This is where you need to pull out the Entrepreneurial Mom's SWOT Analysis so that you can navigate the course of your business, your growth can be consistent and you can keep the momentum by focusing on your customers.

A real estate company I was following experienced tremendous growth in one year. They had newspaper ads, television segments, and several live events. All these methods were beneficial to getting the word out about their business. The business grew very rapidly and developed several satellite offices. A year later, I noticed all the hype was gone and they had a huge turnover in their staff. Many deals from what I had heard through the grapevine went sour. With the huge growth, they lost connection with the people they served and it appeared that they only focused on their revenue gain but not in the value they were in business for—their customers. It is not how rapidly you grow the business, it is about continuing to serve so you will continue to be in business. How do you want to be remembered when someone mentions your business?

Planning for growth begins with having an end in mind. What do you want your business to look like? What resources will you need to get there? Create a timeline and outline the steps you might need to build on to get there. This is similar to the traditional work plan, but what I want you to do is to identify milestones you need to achieve before getting to the next action of growth.

Milestones & Actions	Resources	Who is the most appropriate to complete this?	Timeline	Outcome

Start with your end in mind. What results you want to achieve? Grab some sticky notes and write down what you need for each section above. Place them under each category and move them around to organize your thoughts and to fill in your plan.

Look at what has made your successful to date. Your habits, attitude, and determination, and efforts have led you to where you are today. Concentrate on what is working and continuing doing it. You are in charge and you do not need permission to change or adjust your course. This is your business and life!

Chapter 6

Pay It Forward—Giving Back and Sharing the Wealth

"As we work to create light for others, we naturally light our own way." —**Mary Anne Radmacher**

Have you ever watched a movie trailer and decided you just needed to see that movie? Have you ever read an article and purchased a product or service based on the information you read? Have you ever purchased a toy for your child based on a television commercial?

These are all sneak previews of what is best to come. As people get to know you both on- and off-line, you will get known and remembered for the person you are and what you have to offer. Each article, blog post, video, social media posting, and live event is a trailer for getting to know the person you are and what you have to offer.

By creating a life you love while growing your business and raising a family you are a living example for what others can achieve. You are here for a greater purpose and you are not serving the world by hiding your skills talents or abilities. There are people out there in the world whose life will not be complete until they have interacted with you in some shape or form. What a shame it would be if you did not follow through on your purpose because you lacked the confidence in your abilities to move forward. Imagine that person not reaching their goals because you did not follow through on why you're here.

Do not underestimate the impact you have in the world. In the modern day parable, *The Dream Giver* by Bruce Wilkinson, a boy named Ordinary, leaves the Land of Familiar to pursue his big dream. He searches for what he needs to become: Somebody. But little does he realize that everything he needed already existed within him. He overcomes his fears by having the courage and confidence to go after his big dream. Ordinary started to notice that obstacles were actually opportunities along his journey.

Do not wait for everything to be just perfect before you take action. There will always be different demands you have in your lives. You need to step out of your comfort zone and make what you dream for your business, life, and family real. Everything you need to succeed already exists within you. You must believe it is possible. You must dare to achieve it.

In another great book, *The Alchemist* by Paulo Coelho, the alchemist shares a father's dream. The father has two sons, one a poet and the other a soldier far away from home. The father has a dream that one of his son's words would be repeated for many years to come. Upon awakening from this dream, he is overjoyed as he knows his son's words will become immortal. The father dies while saving a child shortly after having the dream, goes to heaven, and is granted a wish by the angel that was in his dream. His wish was to hear his son's beautiful poetry shared by people for many years to come. The angel shares with him that his son's poetry is cherished by many, but unfortunately his words will be forgotten. Instead, the man discovers it is his soldier-son's words that people will remember.

One day his son is seeking out a man who he knows can heal one of his servants who is near death. The man he seeks is in fact the son of God. The father's son's words to the man are, "My Lord I am not worthy should you come under my roof but only speak a word and he will be healed." His words have been witness for many years in the Bible. The alchemist states that "No matter what someone does he plays a central part of history and he does not even know it."

As a parent, business owner, family member, and friend, you never know how the information, encouragement, and support you provide will affect others. I know that when you put yourself out there and share who you are and how you can help others you wonder if anyone is listening. There is someone reading and listening to your words. You are impacting others. You too will leave a legacy in each person you contact whether it is through an article, book, blog post, or in live conversation.

Giving the Best of YOU

Give your best, one day at a time. Although we all have "bad hair days," we need to give our best each day even when we are not feeling our best. If your best is only half of what you normally give, then that is your best for that day. So be it. Do not be so hard on yourself. Perhaps you need a break. In order to give your best, you must live your best life and this includes taking time out to look after you.

Self-care is so important when growing a business and raising your family. If you are unable to look after yourself, how are you able to give your best and serve the people you're here to serve? What example are you giving to the people around you? Are you as important as your business?

Take time out each day to incorporate getting exercise so you can look and feel your best. When possible, get this out of the way first thing in the morning. Ensure that you are getting a good night sleep so you are alert, creative, and able to take on the day. The more you incorporate what you love to do into your daily life, the closer you are to creating a life you love!

When your focus is on how much you give each day versus how much you can get, you will be on the path to finding true meaning, more happiness, and greater fulfillment.

Get Ready to Receive the Rewards

Even though, you will put in long hours and even some late nights the amount of traction you get being your own boss and growing into your potential will be one of the most fulfilling journeys you can be on. There will come a time when your compounded efforts will come together and you will be at the pinnacle of your business growth. The rewards that you receive come from knowing and charging what your worth. One of the greatest rewards is the pride of ownership knowing that you have made it to this point because of all your hard work, sacrifices, and efforts. The recognition by your peers and fellow entrepreneurs is so satisfying.

Giving is a huge part of being an entrepreneur, but receiving is also an important part. You must learn to accept gifts and rewards graciously, and appreciate those around you. For those followers are the people who have raised you up to the place where you now stand. Even if you have not started to receive your rewards yet, rest assured if you continue to focus on your end result you will be able to get there. One of the greatest rewards that you will have while growing your business and raising your family is that you can celebrate with the ones you love—your spouse and your children.

Gratitude and Abundance

In order to fully appreciate your accomplishments in your business growth, you must acknowledge what you are grateful for. Look for the abundance in your life. There is so much for everyone to tap into, but notice how you are one of the few who is willing to do the work. Those who are willing to do the work will succeed based on their determination and their quest for knowledge and growth.

Gratitude is a significant part of business growth. I firmly believe that when we are grateful for the people who help us achieve the success we desire, we find more to be grateful for. Our success continues to grow in ways we never knew. Have you heard the saying "we teach people how to treat us"? If we come from a place of gratitude for those around us, they too will be grateful for us. I have learned that with each good deed or act of kindness I have done, or thank you card I have sent, they have led to me to being rewarded with testimonials, words of praise, and new clients based on referrals.

To start being grateful as an entrepreneurial mom recognize that your family loves and supports you, that you have customers who need what you can offer them. Without them, you would not be in business. Shouldn't they be treated like a precious gem? If you treat them well or send referrals their way, don't you think they will want to refer you as well? This is the law of reciprocity.

Developing an attitude of gratitude will make the world look a whole lot better, and it will enable you to shift your mindset to positive thinking and discover inner happiness. Have you developed a cynical point of view of the world? Do you find yourself in a state of worry about the current economy with people losing their jobs and even some their homes?

Three attitude shifters: thanks, gratitude, and appreciation. It seems simple enough. The act of being grateful does not have to mean that we are on our knees bowing in worship nor does it mean we only show gratitude or give thanks during the holiday of Thanksgiving. A person can develop a mindset showing gratitude and appreciation for the blessings in their life anytime, anywhere. Starting where you currently are is the best place because it forces you to focus on the present.

Focusing on the present gives you a new perspective of what is going on and allows you to look at the good in a situation, even though your initial thoughts may not be so pleasant. As you take a step back, you may even notice things you never noticed before. You may see how you've contributed to the situation or how you may have dealt with the situation differently. When you develop a more positive mindset, you can neutralize the negative emotions or tainted experiences from your past.

You might be saying to yourself, "What is there to be thankful for?" Maybe you are angry with your spouse or colleague due to a miscommunication. When you are angry, it is hard for you to find joy and happiness in the moments of frustration. Research has shown that you cannot experience two conflicting emotions at the same time. Anger and happiness cannot coexist. You can only be happy or you can angry at any one point in time. The emotion you experience is a choice.

Look for the good in every situation. There is often a lesson. Sometimes we are so focused on where we are going we fail to see where we currently are.

Gratitude must be felt with a sense of sincerity. When someone does something for you, you should not feel like you owe them or need to repay them in some form. To the giver, their gift is in seeing how excited you are about what they have done for you. You do not owe them anything. We are talking about a random act of kindness. Perhaps someone was ill in your family and someone brought you a couple of meals. You could be grateful or give thanks for the meal by simply sending a thank you card recognizing and appreciating their efforts.

You might wonder who and what you should be thankful for. Giving thanks can be as simple as acknowledging people who:

- make your life easier

- teach you new things
- comfort you in tough times
- celebrate with you in the good times
- connect you with others who you need to know
- encourage you to give your best

Whenever you are unsure of what you have to be grateful or thankful for, imagine a problem you do not have and you will be grateful. When I saw Oprah LIVE, she said, "God does not require your belief. He requires you to experience. You are breathing aren't you?" Gratitude is as simple as being grateful for the breath you breathe.

True gratefulness comes from a conscious decision to stop and recognize the abundance in your life. There are many people who do not have the opportunities or the finances to have or do some of the things that you do, but they are extremely grateful for what they have and the joys it brings to their lives.

"Develop an attitude of gratitude, and give thanks for everything that happens to you, knowing that every step forward is a step toward achieving something bigger and better than your current situation." —**Brian Tracy**

Showing appreciation for gifts, acts of kindness, or a kind word gives pleasure to those receiving it just as much as those giving it, if not more. Saying thank you to everyone feels good. There are many benefits to being grateful. Studies have shown that people who are grateful have less stress, better health, better coping strategies, more enthusiasm, more energy, and greater focus. You begin to focus on what matters most. There are many ways to nurture and develop an attitude of gratitude.

Keep a Gratitude Journal

This allows you to see, in black and white, what you are grateful for, especially if you are having a bad day. Spend at least ten minutes at the beginning or end of your day to reflect on what you have to be grateful for. Write down 3-5 things you are grateful for. If you are unsure of what you have to be grateful for, focus on the moment. Take a deep breath and remember there are people who are struggling to breathe. Listen for the sounds around you; there are people who wish they could hear the sweet sound of their child's voice or a bird sing. Savor your supper; there are people who will not any supper tonight. Watch the glory of the sunset, there are people who cannot see. Counting your blessings can be never ending.

Robert Emmons, a professor of psychology at the University of California, Davis, and the author of *Thanks! How the New Science of Gratitude Can Make You Happier*, says that people who keep a gratitude journal report more energy and they tend to exercise an average of 33 percent more each week and sleep a half hour more each night. Keeping a gratitude journal helps create greater balance and harmony in your life. You will also feel that you have more control and be better prepared to handle what life hands you instead feeling like a victim in your life.

You may even keep a gratitude journal about your spouse or partner and give it to them as a gift. Darren Hardy, publisher and editorial director of *SUCCESS Magazine* and the author of *The Compound Effect*, kept a Thanksgiving (Gratitude) Journal about his spouse for one year. Every day he wrote down what he noticed about his wife and gave thanks for. Darren started his project on Thanksgiving and gave it to his wife the following year. She absolutely loved it! Hardy stated that his relationship was deeper and stronger than ever before. When you start taking notice of all the little things around you, bigger shifts occur in how you think about your life. You will start to take notice that you have a life full of abundance.

Send "Happy" Mail

"God gave you a gift of 86,400 seconds today. Have you used one to say "thank you?" —**William A. Ward**

I have heard some people say that they do not have time to send a thank you card or make a phone call. Everyone has the same amount of time; it all depends on how you use it. You can make a choice to give thanks or choose to ignore someone's kindness. You can make a choice to visit or call a loved one or later learn that they may have passed away. We should learn to say thank you as soon as possible, although it's never too late to say thank you. Some people are not even aware that they have had a significant impact in your life. I challenge you to make one phone call or send one note of appreciation to someone who has made a difference in your life. Make sure you explain what they did that made the difference. You could change their life!

I sent a thank you card to my fourth grade teacher for her hard work and dedication. She sent me a card back stating that my card had brought her tears of joy as she had never had a student send her a thank you card so many years after being in class. It was beautiful!

Writing a thank you note or a note of appreciation need not be difficult. There are many cards and e-cards out in the marketplace and on the internet that may say what you want to say. I call this "Happy" mail. Most people's inboxes and mailboxes are full of newsletters, flyers, and bills to be paid. What a nice change to receive a card of thanks or appreciation in your inbox or mailbox. Create cards from your child's artwork or maybe even some of your own. Try to handwrite your cards whenever possible. You might even try calligraphy for that added touch. It does not need to be fancy to be meaningful. I enjoy keeping cards and creating a gratitude wall of all the people who give thanks or appreciate my services. If you own a business, this a great tool to show your customers you appreciate their business. I have also used SendOutCards to send notes of appreciation and make people feel important. It is a great tool. Appreciation can be in the form of a postcard, note card, or email. Would you like to receive Happy Mail?

In the memoir, *365 Thank Yous: The Year a Simple Act of Daily Gratitude Changed My Life*, John Kralik talks about how feeling grateful and writing thank you notes to others turned his life around. His relationships and career were in turmoil. He thanked people for gifts, their friendship, paying their bills on time, and even the way people greeted him every day. He started to take notice of all things around him - big and small. His appreciation started to spread to others around him. Without even realizing it, John Kralik's shift to an attitude of gratitude started changing the world in which he lived.

Happy mail can be sent to anyone. Acknowledge people who have had an impact in your life in some way:

- your children for adding new experiences to your life
- your spouse for loving you even when you have a bad day
- your grandparents for your Christmas gifts
- your parents for the lessons in life they taught you
- your hairdresser or barber
- the clerk at the department store who went out of their way to give you great customer service
- a mentor or coach who encouraged you or gave you advice
- the gas attendant where you fill up with gas
- your doctor for helping you stay healthy
- your dentist for taking care of your smile
- your eye doctor who helps ensure you can see the world
- your co-worker for stepping up to help you meet a deadline
- your neighbour for shovelling your sidewalk or driveway
- the parents of the bride and groom of a wedding you attended for the invitation to experience a wonderful day of witnessing young love
- the mailperson who delivers your mail
- your friend who listens to you vent you issues
- your team mate who set you up for a chance to score
- your teacher for helping you learn a concept
- a boss for encouraging professional development
- the radio host who plays your favourite song or makes you laugh

As you can see, the list could be endless. We are impacted by so many people in our lives each and every day.

Volunteer Your Time and Talents

Chocolate chip cookies, brownies, and banana bread loaves have put smiles on many faces. If you are not one for writing out cards, you may want to bake something and take it to the person you are appreciating and say "thank you." Maybe you are skilled at wood working; you could make a birdhouse or toolbox for someone. If you are not the handy type, you can volunteer your time or talents. You can visit someone in the hospital or invite someone over for a holiday meal that otherwise might be alone. Some people are good at crunching numbers so they may offer to assist with doing taxes or take a position as treasurer on a committee. Extending your gratitude can be made easier by extending your gifts.

Create a Gratitude Board

Cut out pictures or magazine clippings of things you are grateful for. Arrange and paste them on a poster board. Now you can look at your gratitude board as a reminder of the many blessing you have. You can also scrapbook what you are thankful for and create a book of thanks. The process is just like creating a gratitude board except you keep it in a book any time you are having a bad day or feeling ungrateful, review your book. Make sure you store it in a place that you will reference often.

Coupons of Thanks

Homemade gifts are also a big hit. Your gift of thanks does not have to be expensive; you can give thanks on a shoestring budget too. You can acknowledge others by creating coupons of appreciation. Some coupon ideas include:

- free night of babysitting
- ladies night out
- day of golf with the guys or gals

- massage or back rub
- going for a walk together after supper and holding hands
- ESPN night with a supply of snacks and beverage
- Picnic in the park
- Mother and daughter night with manicures and a movie
- Games night with family and friends
- Pizza and movie night with the family at home

Attract More of What You Want in Your Life

"Feeling grateful or appreciative of someone or something in your life actually attracts more of the things that you appreciate and value into your life." —**Christine Northrup, MD, New York Times Best-selling author**

As you start counting your blessings or being thankful, you will notice that there are more things that will enter your life to be grateful for. What an incredible feeling to know that if you just take time to be thankful every day for at least one thing, it could multiply. The "successful" entrepreneurial mom is one that has a grateful heart and expresses it in her everyday existence.

Develop an attitude of gratitude.

The abundance around of us is amazing! You have so many gifts and talents to share, to give, and to be appreciated. There is no one else like you. Your self- worth is beyond all the riches a person can possess. Everyone enjoys feeling loved, valued, and appreciated; it is human nature. We all want to know that we make a difference.

Developing an attitude of gratitude is easy to develop if you practice it regularly. It has been said that it takes at least 21 days to change or develop a habit. Being grateful does not require great monetary wealth.

Take a Ninety Days Attitude of Gratitude Challenge

For the next ninety days, perform an act of thanks, appreciation, or gratitude every day. You may want to try some of the attitude of gratitude techniques that are best for you. Create a ripple effect by asking others to pass on words, acts of kindness, or thank you notes to others they are grateful for with the essence that they too must ask for their gratitude to be shared. The ripple will continue.

Treasure the gifts in your life.

Help others achieve their goals.

Appreciate the gift given to you.

Notice that there are things everywhere to be grateful for

Keep the momentum of the gratitude going.

Say, "Thank you!"

Have you ever tried to change someone? How is that working for you? I know it usually does not work. Instead of trying to change the world around you, change yourself by adopting an attitude of gratitude. You may even be wondering what this has to do with business. I just want to say, it has everything to do with your mindset, your marketing, your relationships, and the person you are. Great things come to people who chose to be great. Ordinary people can do extraordinary things with the power of their mind and the actions and behaviours that follow. You will feel more upbeat and positive. Life's mountain of challenges will become mole hills. Your energy and enthusiasm for life will attract like-minded individuals in which you can build long lasting relationships which help you to grow and prosper. The way in which you change the world can start with two words, "THANK YOU"!

A Final Message from the Author

Thank you for reading this book. It is my sincere hope that I have helped you:

- grow your business with some of the tools and techniques that can boost your credibility, increase your visibility, and attract your ideal clients, and make more money,
- raise your family by creating deeper relationships and memories you will cherish,
- and remember what matters most—your family, and finally
- to create a life you absolutely love.

You deserve it.
Go out and make the world more beautiful!
YOU have only *one* chance to make it great!

I would love to hear this book has helped you:
Email me at Debra@themillionairewoman.com

About the Author

Debra Kasowski is a thought leader, transformational speaker, blogger, and well respected business strategist and coach. She helps individuals, speakers, authors, and small business owners conquer the barriers to their success by achieving clarity, creating an actionable plan through a variety of goal-setting practices.

Debra is the creator of *The Secrets of the Millionaire Woman* audio series which shares the journeys and lessons of successful women, and is the founder of The Millionaire Woman Club which has helped hundreds of entrepreneurial women live rich from the inside out.

Debra holds a Bachelor of Science degree in Nursing from the University of Alberta and has been practicing nursing for the nearly twenty years providing leadership, coaching for performance, and education through a variety of roles. She has combined her passion and love of helping people with her professional speaking and coaching business to help people transform their lives and business.

Debra has been nominated for the Woman of Worth Award and the MOMpreneur Award of Excellence. She has been featured on CTV, CTSTV, and in *Today's Business Woman Magazine* and the online *Healthy, Wealthy, and Wise.* She is the best-selling co-author of *GPS Your Best Life: Charting Your Destination and Getting There in Style.*

To contact Debra Kasowski visit: www.themillionairewoman.com or www.debrakasowski.com

Other Books by Bettie Youngs Book Publishers

On Toby's Terms

Charmaine Hammond

On Toby's Terms is an endearing story of a beguiling creature who teaches his owners that, despite their trying to teach him how to be the dog they want, he is the one to lay out the terms of being the dog he needs to be. This insight would change their lives forever.

"This is a captivating, heartwarming story and we are very excited about bringing it to film." —**Steve Hudis, Producer**

ISBN: 978-0-9843081-4-9 • ePub: 978-1-936332-15-1

The Maybelline Story
And the Spirited Family Dynasty Behind It

Sharrie Williams

A fascinating and inspiring story, a tale both epic and intimate, alive with the clash, the hustle, the music, and dance of American enterprise.

"A richly told story of a forty-year, white-hot love triangle that fans the flames of a major worldwide conglomerate." —**Neil Shulman, Associate Producer,** *Doc Hollywood*

"Salacious! Engrossing! There are certain stories so dramatic, so sordid, that they seem positively destined for film; this is one of them." —*New York Post*

ISBN: 978-0-9843081-1-8 • ePub: 978-1-936332-17-5

It Started with Dracula
The Count, My Mother, and Me

Jane Congdon

The terrifying legend of Count Dracula silently skulking through the Transylvania night may have terrified generations of filmgoers, but the tall, elegant vampire captivated and electrified a young Jane Congdon, igniting a dream to one day see his mysterious land of ancient castles and misty hollows. Four decades later she finally takes her long-awaited trip—never dreaming that it would unearth decades-buried memories, and trigger a life-changing inner journey. A memoir full of surprises, Jane's story is one of hope, love—and second chances.

"An elegantly written and cleverly told story. An electrifying read." —**Diane Bruno, CISION Media**

ISBN: 978-1-936332-10-6 • ePub: 978-1-936332-11-3

The Rebirth of Suzzan Blac

Suzzan Blac

A horrific upbringing and then abduction into the sex slave industry would all but kill Suzzan's spirit to live. But a happy marriage and two children brought love—and forty-two stunning paintings, art so raw that it initially frightened even the artist. "I hid the pieces for 15 years," says Suzzan, "but just as with the secrets in this book, I am slowing sneaking them out, one by one by one." Now a renowned artist, her work is exhibited world-wide. A story of inspiration, truth and victory.

"A solid memoir about a life reconstructed. Chilling, thrilling, and thought provoking."
—**Pearry Teo, Producer,** *The Gene Generation*

ISBN: 978-1-936332-22-9 • ePub: 978-1-936332-23-6

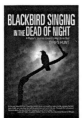

Blackbird Singing in the Dead of Night
What to Do When God Won't Answer

Gregory L. Hunt

Pastor Greg Hunt had devoted nearly thirty years to congregational ministry, helping people experience God and find their way in life. Then came his own crisis of faith and calling. While turning to God for guidance, he finds nothing. Neither his education nor his religious involvements could prepare him for the disorienting impact of the experience. Alarmed, he tries an experiment. The result is startling—and changes his life entirely.

"Compelling. If you have ever longed to hear God whispering a love song into your life, read this book." —**Gary Chapman,** *NY Times* **bestselling author,** *The Love Languages of God*

ISBN: 978-1-936332-07-6 • ePub: 978-1-936332-18-2

Fastest Man in the World
The Tony Volpentest Story

Tony Volpentest
Foreword by Ross Perot

Tony Volpentest, a four-time Paralympic gold medalist and five-time world champion sprinter, is a 2012 nominee for the Olympic Hall of Fame. This inspirational story details his being born without feet, to holding records as the fastest sprinter in the world.

"This inspiring story is about the thrill of victory to be sure—winning gold—but it is also a reminder about human potential: the willingness to push ourselves beyond the ledge of our own imagination. A powerfully inspirational story." —**Charlie Huebner, United States Olympic Committee**

ISBN: 978-1-936332-00-7 • ePub: 978-1-936332-01-4

DON CARINA: *WWII Mafia Heroine*

Ron Russell

A father's death in Southern Italy in the 1930s—a place where women who can read are considered unfit for marriage—thrusts seventeen-year-old Carina into servitude as a "black widow," a legal head of the household who cares for her twelve siblings. A scandal forces her into a marriage to Russo, the "Prince of Naples." By cunning force, Carina seizes control of Russo's organization and disguising herself as a man, controls the most powerful of Mafia groups for nearly a decade.

"A woman as the head of the Mafia who shows her family her resourcefulness, strength and survival techniques. Unique, creative and powerful! This exciting book blends history, intrigue and power into one delicious epic adventure that you will not want to put down!" —**Linda Gray, Actress, *Dallas***

ISBN: 978-0-9843081-9-4 • ePub: 978-1-936332-49-6

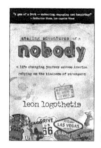

Amazing Adventures of a Nobody

Leon Logothetis

From the Hit Television Series Aired in 100 Countries!

Tired of his disconnected life and uninspiring job, Leon Logothetis leaves it all behind—job, money, home, even his cell phone—and hits the road with nothing but the clothes on his back and five dollars in his pocket, relying on the kindness of strangers and the serendipity of the open road for his daily keep. Masterful story-telling!

"A gem of a book; endearing, engaging and inspiring." —**Catharine Hamm, Los Angeles Times Travel Editor**

ISBN: 978-0-9843081-3-2 • ePub: 978-1-936332-51-9

MR. JOE
Tales from a Haunted Life

Joseph Barnett and Jane Congdon

Do you believe in ghosts? Joseph Barnett didn't, until the winter he was fired from his career job and became a school custodian. Assigned the graveyard shift, Joe was confronted with a series of bizarre and terrifying occurrences.

"Thrilling, thoughtful, elegantly told. So much more than a ghost story." —**Cyrus Webb, CEO, Conversation Book Club**

ISBN: 978-1-936332-78-6 • ePub: 978-1-936332-79-3

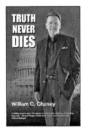

Truth Never Dies

William C. Chasey

A lobbyist for some 40 years, William C. Chasey represented some of the world's most prestigious business clients and twenty-three foreign governments before the US Congress. His integrity never questioned. All that changed when Chasey was hired to forge communications between Libya and the US Congress. A trip he took with a US Congressman for discussions with then Libyan leader Muammar Qadhafi forever changed Chasey's life. Upon his return, his bank accounts were frozen, clients and friends had been advised not to take his calls.

Things got worse: the CIA, FBI, IRS, and the Federal Judiciary attempted to coerce him into using his unique Libyan access to participate in a CIA-sponsored assassination plot of the two Libyans indicted for the bombing of Pan Am flight 103. Chasey's refusal to cooperate resulted in a six-year FBI investigation and sting operation, financial ruin, criminal charges, and incarceration in federal prison.

ISBN: 978-1-936332-46-5 • ePub: 978-1-936332-47-2

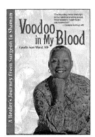

Voodoo in My Blood
A Healer's Journey from Surgeon to Shaman

Carolle Jean-Murat, M.D.

Born and raised in Haiti to a family of healers, US trained physician Carolle Jean-Murat came to be regarded as a world-class surgeon. But her success harbored a secret: in the operating room, she could quickly intuit the root cause of her patient's illness, often times knowing she could help the patient without surgery. Carolle knew that to fellow surgeons, her intuition was best left unmentioned. But when the devastating earthquake hit Haiti and Carolle returned to help, she had to acknowledge the shaman she had become.

"This fascinating memoir sheds light on the importance of asking yourself, 'Have I created for myself the life I've meant to live?'" —**Christiane Northrup, M.D., author of the New York Times bestsellers:** *Women's Bodies, Women's Wisdom*

ISBN: 978-1-936332-05-2 • ePub: 978-1-936332-04-5

Electric Living
The Science behind the Law of Attraction

Kolie Crutcher

An electrical engineer by training, Crutcher applies his in-depth knowledge of electrical engineering principles and practical engineering experience detailing the scientific explanation of why human beings become what they think. A practical, step-by-step guide to help you harness your thoughts and emotions so that the Law of Attraction will benefit you.

ISBN: 978-1-936332-58-8 • ePub: 978-1-936332-59-5

Hostage of Paradox: *A Qualmish Disclosure*

John Rixey Moore

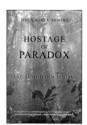

Few people then or now know about the clandestine war that the CIA ran in Vietnam, using the Green Berets for secret operations throughout Southeast Asia. This was not the Vietnam War of the newsreels, the body counts, rice paddy footage, and men smoking cigarettes on the sandbag bunkers. This was a shadow directive of deep-penetration interdiction, reconnaissance, and assassination missions conducted by a selected few Special Forces units, deployed quietly from forward operations bases to prowl through agendas that, for security reasons, were seldom understood by the men themselves.

Hostage of Paradox is the first-hand account by one of these elite team leaders.

"Deserving of a place in the upper ranks of Vietnam War memoirs." —**Kirkus Review**

"Read this book, you'll be, as John Moore puts it, 'transfixed, like kittens in a box.'" —**David Willson, Book Review, The VVA Veteran**

ISBN: 978-1-936332-37-3 • ePub: 978-1-936332-33-5

Living with Multiple Personalities
The Christine Ducommun Story

Christine Ducommun

Christine Ducommun was a happily married wife and mother of two, when—after moving back into her childhood home—she began to experience panic attacks and bizarre flashbacks. Eventually diagnosed with Dissociative Identity Disorder (DID), Christine's story details an extraordinary twelve-year ordeal unraveling the buried trauma of her forgotten past.

"Reminiscent of the Academy Award-winning *A Beautiful Mind,* this true story will have you on the edge of your seat. Spellbinding!" —**Josh Miller, Producer**

ISBN: 978-0-9843081-5-6 • ePub: 978-1-936332-06-9

The Tortoise Shell Code

V Frank Asaro

Off the coast of Southern California, the Sea Diva, a tuna boat, sinks. Members of the crew are missing and what happened remains a mystery. Anthony Darren, a renowned and wealthy lawyer at the top of his game, knows the boat's owner and soon becomes involved in the case. As the case goes to trial, a missing crew member is believed to be at fault, but new evidence comes to light and the finger of guilt points in a completely unanticipated direction. An action-packed thriller.

ISBN: 978-1-936332-60-1 • ePub: 978-1-936332-61-8

Out of the Transylvania Night

Aura Imbarus
A Pulitzer-Prize entry

"I'd grown up in the land of Transylvania, homeland to Dracula, Vlad the Impaler, and worse, dictator Nicolae Ceausescu," writes the author. "Under his rule, like vampires, we came to life after sundown, hiding our heirloom jewels and documents deep in the earth." Fleeing to the US to rebuild her life, she discovers a startling truth about straddling two cultures and striking a balance between one's dreams and the sacrifices that allow a sense of "home."

"Aura's courage shows the degree to which we are all willing to live lives centered on freedom, hope, and an authentic sense of self. Truly a love story!" —**Nadia Comaneci, Olympic Champion**

ISBN: 978-0-9843081-2-5 • ePub: 978-1-936332-20-5

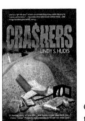

Crashers
A Tale of "Cappers" and "Hammers"

Lindy S. Hudis

The illegal business of fraudulent car accidents is a multi-million dollar racket, involving unscrupulous medical providers, personal injury attorneys, and the cooperating passengers involved in the accidents. Innocent people are often swept into it. Newly engaged Nathan and Shari, who are swimming in mounting debt, were easy prey: seduced by an offer from a stranger to move from hard times to good times in no time, Shari finds herself the "victim" in a staged auto accident. Shari gets her payday, but breaking free of this dark underworld will take nothing short of a miracle.

"A riveting story of love, life—and limits. A non-stop thrill ride." —**Dennis "Danger" Madalone, stunt coordinator, *Castle***

ISBN: 978-1-936332-27-4 • ePub: 978-1-936332-28-1

The Ten Commandments for Travelers

Nancy Chappie

Traveling can be an overwhelming experience fraught with delays, tension, and unexpected complications. But whether you're traveling for business or pleasure, alone or with family or friends, there are things you can do to make your travels more enjoyable—even during the most challenging experiences. Easy to implement tips for hassle-free travel, and guidance for those moments that threaten to turn your voyage into an unpleasant experience. You'll learn how to avoid extra costs and aggravations, save time, and stay safe; how to keep your cool under the worst of circumstances, how to embrace new cultures, and how to fully enjoy each moment you're on the road.

ISBN: 978-1-936332-74-8 • ePub: 978-1-936332-75-5

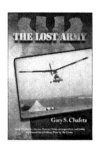

The Search for the Lost Army
The National Geographic and
Harvard University Expedition

Gary S. Chafetz

In one of history's greatest ancient disasters, a Persian army of 50,000 soldiers was suffocated by a hurricane-force sandstorm in 525 BC in Egypt's Western Desert. No trace of this conquering army, hauling huge quantities of looted gold and silver, has ever surfaced.

Gary Chafetz, referred to as "one of the ten best journalists of the past twenty-five years," is a former Boston Globe correspondent and was twice nominated for a Pulitzer Prize by the Globe.

ISBN: 978-1-936332-98-4 • ePub: 978-1-936332-99-1

A World Torn Asunder
The Life and Triumph of Constantin C. Giurescu

Marina Giurescu, M.D.

Constantin C. Giurescu was Romania's leading historian and author. His granddaughter's fascinating story of this remarkable man and his family follows their struggles in war-torn Romania from 1900 to the fall of the Soviet Union. An "enlightened" society is dismantled with the 1946 Communist takeover of Romania, and Constantin is confined to the notorious Sighet penitentiary. Drawing on her grandfather's prison diary (which was put in a glass jar, buried in a yard, then smuggled out of the country by Dr. Paul E. Michelson—who does the FOREWORD for this book), private letters and her own research, Dr. Giurescu writes of the legacy from the turn of the century to the fall of Communism.

We see the rise of modern Romania, the misery of World War I, the blossoming of its culture between the wars, and then the sellout of Eastern Europe to Russia after World War II. In this sweeping account, we see not only its effects socially and culturally, but the triumph in its wake: a man and his people who reclaim better lives for themselves, and in the process, teach us a lesson in endurance, patience, and will—not only to survive, but to thrive.

"The inspirational story of a quiet man and his silent defiance in the face of tyranny."
—**Dr. Connie Mariano, author of *The White House Doctor***

ISBN: 978-1-936332-76-2 • ePub: 978-1-936332-77-9

Diary of a Beverly Hills Matchmaker

Marla Martenson

Quick-witted Marla takes her readers for a hilarious romp through her days as an LA matchmaker where looks are everything and money talks. The Cupid of Beverly Hills has introduced countless couples who lived happily ever-after, but for every success story there are hysterically funny dating disasters with high-maintenance, out of touch clients. Marla writes with charm and self-effacement about the universal struggle to love and be loved.

ISBN 978-0-9843081-0-1 • ePub: 978-1-936332-03-8

123

Thank You for Leaving Me
Finding Divinity and Healing in Divorce

Farhana Dhalla
Foreword by Neale Donald Walsch

The end of any relationship, especially divorce, can leave us bereft, feeling unmoored, empty. Speaking to that part of our hearts that knows you must find your way to a new and different place, this compassionate book of words of wisdom helps grow this glimmering knowledge—and offers hope and healing for turning this painful time into one of renewal and rediscovery. This book is balm for your wounded heart, and can help you turn your fragility to endurable coping, and will you rediscover your inner strengths. Best of all, this book will help you realize the transformative power inherent in this transition.

ISBN: 978-1-936332-85-4 • ePub: 978-1-936332-86-1

GPS YOUR BEST LIFE
Charting Your Destination and Getting There in Style

Charmaine Hammond and Debra Kasowski
Foreword by Jack Canfield

A most useful guide to charting and traversing the many options that lay before you.

"A perfect book for servicing your most important vehicle: yourself. No matter where you are in your life, the concepts and direction provided in this book will help you get to a better place. It's a must read." —**Ken Kragen, author of** *Life Is a Contact Sport*, **and organizer of** *We Are the World*, **and** *Hands Across America*, **and other historic humanitarian events**

ISBN: 978-1-936332-26-7 • ePub: 978-1-936332-41-0

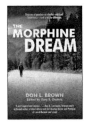

The Morphine Dream

Don Brown with *Pulitzer nominated Gary S. Chafetz*

At 36, high-school dropout and a failed semi-professional ballplayer Donald Brown hit bottom when an industrial accident left him immobilized. But Brown had a dream while on a morphine drip after surgery: he imagined himself graduating from Harvard Law School (he was a classmate of Barack Obama) and walking across America. Brown realizes both seemingly unreachable goals, and achieves national recognition as a legal crusader for minority homeowners. An intriguing tale of his long walk—both physical and metaphorical. A story of perseverance and second chances. Sheer inspiration for those wishing to reboot their lives.

"An incredibly inspirational memoir." —**Alan M. Dershowitz, professor, Harvard Law School**

ISBN: 978-1-936332-25-0 • ePub: 978-1-936332-39-7

Cinderella and the Carpetbagger

Grace Robbins

Harold Robbins's steamy books were once more widely read than the Bible. His novels sold more than 750 million copies and created the sex-power-glamour genre of popular literature that would go on to influence authors from Jackie Collins and Jacqueline Susann to TV shows like Dallas and Dynasty. What readers don't know is that Robbins—whom the media had dubbed the "prince of sex and scandal"—actually "researched" the free-wheeling escapades depicted in his books himself . . . along with his drop-dead, gorgeous wife, Grace. Now, in this revealing tell-all, for the first time ever, Grace Robbins rips the covers off the real life of the international best-selling author.

The 1960s and '70s were decades like no others—radical, experimental, libertine. Grace Robbins chronicles the rollicking good times, peppering her memoir with anecdotes of her encounters with luminaries from the world of entertainment and the arts—not to mention most of Hollywood. The couple was at the center of a globetrotting jet set, with mansions in Beverly Hills, villas and yachts on the French Riviera and Acapulco. Their life rivaled—and often surpassed—that of the characters in his books. Champagne flowed, cocaine was abundant, and sex in the pre-AIDS era was embraced with abandon. Along the way, the couple agreed to a "modern marriage," that Harold insisted upon. With charm, introspection, and humor, Grace lays open her fascinating, provocative roller-coaster ride of a life—her own true Cinderella tale.

"This sweet little memoir's getting a movie deal." —**New York Post**

"I gulped down every juicy minute of this funny, outrageous memoir. Do not take a pill before you go to bed with this book, because you will not be able to put it down until the sun comes up." —**Rex Reed**

"Grace Robbins has written an explosive tell-all. Sexy fun." —**Jackie Collins**

"You have been warned. This book is VERY HOT!" —**Robin Leach, Lifestyles of the Rich & Famous**

ISBN: 978-0-9882848-2-1 • ePub: 978-0-9882848-4-5

The Girl Who Gave Her Wish Away

Sharon Babineau
Foreword by Craig Kielburger

The Children's Wish Foundation approached lovely thirteen-year-old Maddison Babineau just after she received her cancer diagnosis. "You can have anything," they told her, "a Disney cruise? The chance to meet your favorite movie star? A five thousand dollar shopping spree?"

Maddie knew exactly what she wanted. She had recently been moved to tears after watching a television program about the plight of orphaned children. Maddie's wish? To ease the suffering of these children half-way across the world. Despite the ravishing cancer, she became an indefatigable fundraiser for "her children." In The Girl Who Gave Wish Away, her mother reveals Maddie's remarkable journey of providing hope and future to the village children who had filled her heart.

A special story, heartwarming and reassuring.

ISBN: 978-1-936332-96-0 • ePub: 978-1-936332-97-7

Company of Stone

John Rixey Moore

With yet unhealed wounds from recent combat, John Moore undertook an unexpected walking tour in the rugged Scottish highlands. With the approach of a season of freezing rainstorms he took shelter in a remote monastery—a chance encounter that would change his future, his beliefs about blind chance, and the unexpected courses by which the best in human nature can smuggle its way into the life of a stranger. Afterwards, a chance conversation overheard in a village pub steered him to Canada, where he took a job as a rock drill operator in a large industrial gold mine. The dangers he encountered among the lost men in that dangerous other world, secretive men who sought permanent anonymity in the perils of work deep underground—a brutal kind of monasticism itself—challenged both his endurance and his sense of humanity.

With sensitivity and delightful good humor, Moore explores the surprising lessons learned in these strangely rich fraternities of forgotten men—a brotherhood housed in crumbling medieval masonry, and one shared in the unforgiving depths of the gold mine.

ISBN: 978-1-936332-44-1 • ePub: 978-1-936332-45-8

Trafficking the Good Life

Jennifer Myers

Jennifer Myers had worked hard toward a successful career as a dancer in Chicago. But just as her star was rising, she fell for the kingpin of a drug trafficking operation. Drawn to his life of excitement, she soon acquiesced to driving marijuana across the country, making easy money she stacked in shoeboxes and spent like an heiress. Only time in a federal prison made her face up to and understand her choices. It was there, at rock bottom, that she discovered that her real prison was the one she had unwittingly made inside herself and where she could start rebuilding a life of purpose and ethical pursuit.

"In her gripping memoir Jennifer Myers offers a startling account of how the pursuit of an elusive American Dream can lead us to the depths of the American criminal underbelly. Her book is as much about being human in a hyper-materialistic society as it is about drug culture. When the DEA finally knocks on Myers' door, she and the reader both see the moment for what it truly is—not so much an arrest as a rescue." **—Tony D'Souza, author of *Whiteman and Mule***

ISBN: 978-1-936332-67-0 • ePub: 978-1-936332-68-7

Universal Co-opetition
Nature's Fusion of Co-operation and Competition

V Frank Asaro

A key ingredient in personal and business success is competition—and cooperation. Too much of one or the other can erode personal and organizational goals. This book identifies and explains the natural, fundamental law that unifies the apparently opposing forces of cooperation and competition.

ISBN: 978-1-936332-08-3 • ePub: 978-1-936332-09-0

Bettie Youngs Books

We specialize in MEMOIRS

. . . books that celebrate

fascinating people and

remarkable journeys

In bookstores everywhere, online, Espresso,
or from the publisher, Bettie Youngs Books
VISIT OUR WEBSITE AT
www.BettieYoungsBooks.com
To contact:
info@BettieYoungsBooks.com

CPSIA information can be obtained at www.ICGtesting.com
Printed in the USA
LVOW13s0341051113

359968LV00001B/33/P